M000040465

The Secret

Behind

The Secret
Law of Attraction

The Secret
Behind
The Secret
Law of Attraction

They Didn't Want You to Know.
You'll Be Shocked, Startled and Amazed.
Love and Success or
Failure and Self Destruction,
are Within...
It's not What You Thought
It's the Real Secret Behind the Secret

Bob Beverley, Dave Lakhani
Blair Warren, Kevin Hogan

Copyright 2007
Network 3000 Publishing
All Rights Reserved

The Secret Behind The Secret Law of Attraction
Authors:
Kevin Hogan
Bob Beverley
Dave Lakhani
Blair Warren

Includes Bibliographic References

ISBN: 1-934266-02-7
ISBN: 978-1-934266-02-1

Self-Help Techniques

Printed in the United States of America
Network 3000 Publishing
3432 Denmark Avenue #108
Eagan, Minnesota 55123
USA
(612) 616-0732

Dedication from Bob Beverley

To Cindy, Laura, Michelle and Aaron
--my treasures.

Dedication from Kevin Hogan

Katie, Mark and Jessica

Dedication from Dave Lakhani

To my beautiful daughter Austria who makes me think and challenge my thinking every day. And to my wife Stephanie who thinks more amazing things in a minute than I'll think in my whole life. And, to Kevin, Bob and Blair, thank you for standing on the edge with me!

And to every person who ever had the courage to listen, think and stand up and say "That doesn't make sense!"

Dedication from Blair Warren

For Claudia, Samantha, and Zachary.
I would be lost without you - and that's no secret.

Acknowledgements

Bob Beverley

I would especially like to acknowledge the influence of Dr. Malcolm Reid, who is retiring this year as Professor of Philosophy, Gordon College, Wenham, Mass. He taught all of his students, including me, to sit up straight in our chairs and endeavor to really think. His kind spirit, infectious laugh, and warm, reasonable faith made philosophy a bit easier--but we still had to think and think again. Thank you, Dr. Reid.

Kevin Hogan

Mark Hogan for providing me with my energy boosts every day of the week. Katie Hogan, Jessica Hogan. For those people who are there: Ken Owens, Michelle Drum, Lisa McLellan, Jennifer Battaglino, Ron Stubbs, Meredith Kaplan, Devin and Rachel Hastings, Elsom Eldridge, Scott and Carmen Schluter. Thanks to my co-authors of this book. Three great men. My friends around the world, you know who you are.

Blair Warren

I'd like to thank my friends Pat Brozinsky, "Cosmic Connie" Schmidt, Tony Michalski, Ben Mack and Tony Blake for their help on this project. They not only provided me with valuable information and insights, but also kept me motivated and laughing along the way. And a special thanks to my co-authors for inviting me to work alongside them on this book. I have the greatest respect for each of them and am honored to be included in their company.

CONTENTS

Introduction

Its followers believe it is the secret formula, known through the ages by various philosophers and mystics and scientists, that guarantees easy access to the success we've always dreamed of. And so they say, "enough is enough" to the ignorant, blind, obstacle-ridden, hard life that millions of people are living. Live The Secret and you will bypass the unnecessary frustrations, long learning curves, and tortuous detours that seem to have humanity by the throat.

The Secret is THE way. It's a scientifically proven universal law that always works in every situation, every time.

"Most men lead lives of quiet desperation", said Thoreau, and THE SECRET shouts passionately that this does not have to be. There is true magic afoot, there are lanterns to be lit, passions to be embraced, secret thoughts to be learned—and we can discover a whole new way of living that is, simply, there for the taking!

And now there are those who see real and grave danger in this virus that is spreading through the English-speaking world...and they say, "enough is enough."

The leaders of The Secret crossed the line of humanity and compassion when they began to state that people bring on their own illnesses, cause their own genocide, rape and murder.

From the "official course of The Secret": *"Do communities that are victims of crime waves or war attract these...? The answer is YES - ... "Group Manifestation".*

Groups of people can manifest group destiny through their thoughts and their thoughts ALONE.

That was an eye opener for authors of this book…but there are a lot of other people out there in the world that have more to share with you and me…

They say THE SECRET is not a secret. It has all been said before and, in every generation, its salespeople have made a ton of money, garnished up some following, or had their moments of fame-- and eventually humanity came to its senses and bypassed any movement that offered a quick fix and easy, "insider" answers to the perennial struggles on earth's difficult shores.

And what about the authors of this book? Are we saying, "enough is enough"? Well, you will have to obtain the real secret within…we did a little bit of digging and have found out the real truth about The Secret. We've found that all that glitters is not gold. You'll have to make your own decision.

What we can promise is that we will do our best to be fair, open-minded, kind, truthful and honest. Any mistakes in the text will be repaired in the next edition of the book. Our purpose is to accurately represent The Secret and then show how and why we are concerned for the poor and defenseless.

And whether you agree with us or not, you will find out some things that really do matter about the human mind and heart. And we're going to show you how the people who supposedly had "The Secret" through the ages, really felt about philosophies like The Secret. The geniuses that the movie and books claim "had the Secret" were indeed some of the greatest thinkers of the last two thousand years….but is it true that they "had the Secret" or believed anything like the Secret? In this book we'll show you what they REALLY wrote and how they thought….and then we'll examine feelings and possibly take issue with what people say are the dangerous aspects of The Secret.

And you'll find out what people *can really* do to make their life better.

In short, it is our sincere hope that this book will have its own sort of magic— if only by illustrating the magic of understanding and the universally-needed secret act of respecting those with whom we differ and having compassion and love toward all.

Bob Beverley
Kevin Hogan
Dave Lakhani
Blair Warren

Chapter One
What Is The Secret and Its History?
(BB)

The Secret is out. As of this writing, 3 million people have bought the book, 1.25 million have purchased the DVD, and millions more heard it explained on Oprah and Larry King Live. Chatter about The Secret is ablaze on the Internet and it has become a huge topic of debate in the self-help world. The Secret has earned full-page coverage in the New York Times, a cover story in Newsweek, and continued top billing on prime time news journalism. The controversy and intrigue surrounding The Secret is growing exponentially.

The Secret is, first of all, the title of a book and DVD by Reality TV Show Producer, Rhonda Byrne. In this book she discloses, with the help of others, that The Secret is a truth about the universe and human beings that has been known by only a select few through the centuries.

We are told very quickly at the start of the DVD that, "The Secret is The Law of Attraction."

This Law is based on the notion that the laws of physics show us that "like attracts like" and, therefore, we human beings attract everything that ever happens to us.

The Law of Attraction applies to everyone without exception. This Law is viewed as the secret key to success and this key is available equally and easily to everyone. In a very focused, personal and individual way, this Law is about each of us.

15

Everything comes to us because we attract it.

Thoughts become things, and as we emit our thoughts and feelings the Universe sends back the corresponding reality.

For example, if we are in debt and feel bad about it, we attract debt from the universe. If we desire wealth, the Universe will send it our way. This law works with every person and it is always operating. Negative attracts negative, positive attracts positive— "the Law of Attraction is really obedient", says one speaker.

"The Universe is a catalog where we pick out what we want and ask for it", says another expert.

In short, ***"You draw everything to yourself that ever happened to you. This is the Secret."***

It is literally a "Your wish is your command" universe. We ask, believe, "feel good about it" and are "open to receive" whatever we get.

"Place your order with the universe. It's as easy as that. The Universe will start to rearrange itself."

Expect a bill and you will get it. Expect a check and it will show up. The past is who you were—change what you want and "current reality will begin to change".

The Secret places great emphasis on ***gratitude*** because when you focus on lack, you attract more of what you don't have.

A second emphasis is on **visualization** because you need to practice seeing what you desire. You can practice with a cup of coffee, a parking space, reacquainting with old friends, and then move on to bigger and better things. A third emphasis is on

16

intention because we can become the solution in this universe of abundance.

There is a third emphasis on the **internal world of people**—our minds, but especially our feelings—as well as on being positive.

In fact, advocates of the Secret insist that even our negative thoughts about something bad increases its reality because "we add our energy to bad stuff. It creates resistance."

In this sense, the anti-war movement creates war. In this regard, Mother Theresa is cited because she said she would go to a pro-peace rally, not an anti-war protest. (We actually have no record of such a statement by Mother Theresa but this is one of many unsubstantiated quotes, attributions and claims by authors and actors in The Secret.)

Every speaker involved with The Secret looks healthy, happy, and positive.

We would expect no less of a troupe that thinks "life is phenomenal" and we *all* can "go anywhere, do anything, achieve anything" as long as we want to attract it.

In America and Australia, where The Secret has really taken off, we are not used to movements and religions where we are so easily included. We are usually told that we have to join something, study something, and possibly even give up something, and believe a whole lot of other things. Any sort of secret is often obscure, difficult to understand, and involves an authority figure who has greater access to the inner workings of the mystery.

But The Secret is gloriously different. The key to the universe is not in another country or in a wealthy gated community. It is not inside a guru who you have to find at the top of a mountain.

17

Finally, its followers say, there is a secret that you can easily access because The Secret is inside you. You have deep desires for health, wealth, success, and you have all kinds of unique dreams that are at the heart of your particular journey. These, says The Secret, are the most attractive things about you.

But according to teachers of The Secret, there is one problem: you probably do not realize this potential in you, because your mind and heart have been corroded by despair, bills, envy, doubt, limiting beliefs, negativity and ingratitude.

And if you cannot see this secret inside you, how can you ever see the corresponding magic at the heart of the Universe? And what is this parallel secret, which speaks of a reality that wants to bond with you in an intimate dance of success and growth and arrival? It is simply and wonderfully this: the Universe wants you to succeed in living the life of passion and bliss that, heretofore, has escaped your notice.

Advocates of The Secret have discovered that the Law of Attraction is really all you need to make your dreams come true. They claim that this Law has always been in existence, but though it has been noticed by some, and lived by many, it is only at this point in time that word is really getting out.

With the assistance of modern day technology (Internet, TV, DVD and CD's), Rhonda Bryne and Jerry and Esther Hicks have persistently spread the word. These three people do not claim to have invented The Secret or the Law of Attraction.

They claim that the Law of Attraction is a universal law like gravity or the 2nd Law of Thermodynamics and the need for germ free surgery. These are truths, facts and laws that have always existed—but that have awaited our discovery and our embrace.

The Secret book and DVD informs us that Plato, Jesus, Shakespeare, Beethoven, Lincoln, Hugo, Churchill and Einstein knew The Secret.

It is implied that wealthy people and other coteries have kept the secret hidden for themselves. The movie tells us The Secret was banished.

At the fast pace beginning of the movie we are informed that the Secret has been "buried....coveted...suppressed" but it is here now for the taking.

And modern day marketers, self-help gurus, motivational speakers and new age visionaries have added their testimonies and teachings to this (in their eyes) much needed movement.

The team of experts cited in the movie and book also include psychologists, physicists, investment bankers, ministers, and a doctor. (Even when it turns out they may not be what they say they are…)

We are told that two of the people featured in the movie used the Law of Attraction to heal themselves:

Cathy Goodman of a total healing of breast cancer in 3 months, without chemo or radiation. And Morris Goodman, "The Miracle Man" who fought back from spinal paralysis to a normal life. Both emphasized the power of the mind, and explained how they saturated their thoughts with the positive outcome.

A few historical figures are quoted by voice over or text: Carl Jung, Winston Churchill, Martin Luther King Jr. Henry Ford, Joseph Campbell, Emerson, Alexander Graham Bell, W. Clement Stone and Robert Collier.

19

All in all, if we can have "truth by association" then The Secret has some fine associates making cameo appearances in the film.

"Go anywhere, do anything, achieve anything" is the promised result of The Secret.

Who would not want such a life?

Many claim they have "found it" and are "pro-Secret." Many find The Secret too good to be true—and very pernicious in its attitude towards the sick, the abused, the raped, the victims of genocide, the oppressed.

Others argue that none of the famous people thought, believed or wrote anything like The Secret or The Law of Attraction.

For example, the Producer of The Secret didn't quote Churchill accurately. Churchill literally abhorred metaphysics and metaphysical thinking. The quote used in The Secret is what his COUSINS were trying to persuade him of, and Churchill turned around and said it was "absurd."

If there was just one of these "mistakes," you could understand…but if there is a host of misleading references and false associations….

That's disingenuous at best and fraudulent at worst.

We will look at both sides of the coin of The Secret…in this book.

And just what IS The Secret?

Here are the words of those who teach The Secret…from the official Secret website:

(http://freeyourdreams.theofficialsecretseminar.com).

The 2nd lesson defines, "The Law of Attraction and Facing Responsibility for Who and Where You Are Today."

Here are some brief excerpts from the "lesson":

"Whatever is going on in your mind you are attracting to you."

"Whatever you think about, whether it's good or bad - you attract into your life. Whether you want it or not is irrelevant - think about something you DON'T WANT and you attract it into your life."

"Unconscious attraction is what happens when we let our uncontrolled thoughts run free. Worry about getting out of debt - and that's what you attract - MORE debt."

"Worry about getting old - and you'll start experiencing the effects of old age."

"There's a simple formula we want you to understand:
Thought + Emotion = Attraction."

"It's easier to attract the good than to attract the bad."

"Accept responsibility for where you are today...or you'll be powerless to change."

"The Key to understanding the Law of Attraction is to understand that you are responsible for everything in your life. EVERYTHING. At some level - consciously or unconsciously, you attracted every person, every job, every idea, every illness, every joy and every bit of pain into your life."

"Do communities that are victims of crime waves or war attract these...? The answer is YES – Group Manifestation."

Next we've quoted the spirit beings Abraham, Rhonda Byrne, Byrne's subordinates, in that order. Because Byrne learned from "Abraham," we've chosen to default to the spirit being where I have conflicting information from Byrne and her subordinates.

"The Law of Attraction is a Scientific Fact. It 'works' 100% of the time, all the time."

"The universe is interconnected."

"Everything is energy."

"Even people are energy."

"Like attracts like."

"Your thoughts are energy."

"Your brain sends out thoughts which are magnetic."

"People have a vibration."

"That vibration goes into the universe."

"Magnetically, physical things (anything because everything is energy) come to your environment because of the vibration and the Law."

"Ultimately whatever you are vibrating is what you get."

"Thinking causes emotions and emotions cause vibrations which attract."

"Everything draws to itself that which is like itself."

"We are all God, God is all of us."

"We are all Vibrational Beings. You're like a receiving mechanism that when you set your tuner to the station, you're going to hear what's playing. Whatever you are focused upon is the way you set your tuner, and when you focus there for as little as 17 seconds, you activate that vibration within you. Once you activate a vibration within you, **Law of Attraction** *begins responding to that vibration, and you're off and running--whether it's something wanted or unwanted"* --- Abraham
Excerpted from the workshop in North Los Angeles, CA on Sunday, August 18th, 2002

The Secret's author, Rhonda Byrne, indicates that the country of Rwanda brought their rape, murder and genocide upon themselves.

The official course for learning The Secret confirms that there is group attraction and that "communities" can attract very bad things.

"It's as easy to attract $1 as it is $10,000."

See, Believe, Receive is the three-step formula from Byrne.

(Note: One person under Byrne uses a different formula, See, Feel, Act.)

Byrne's interpretation of The Law of Attraction comes from her "relationship" with the disembodied spirit Abraham and channeling (Esther Hicks) and having read their books.

Similar philosophies to the Law of Attraction have come up in the past including Jesus saying, "Whatever you ask in my name, it shall be done."

23

"What comes to you...the experiences of your life are brought."

To "use" the Law of Attraction, you fix your mind on something and it will come to you.

"Think of a feather, a feather will come."

"It's just as easy to attract $10,000 as it is $1."

Chapter Two
The Public Response to The Secret
(BB)

"There are two kinds of people in the world: those who divide the world in two and those who do not"
Anonymous

Many people say that The Secret has changed their lives. Many more are enthusiastic about its possibilities for their lives, and endorse the movies, books, CD's, and speakers associated with the Law of Attraction.

As of April 1, 2007 we read every review associated with The Secret Extended Version DVD on Amazon.com to see how people were receiving the Secret. How is the public reacting to the movie?

Here are our findings among those with a positive reception:

Many say that they already knew about the Secret. It reminded them to refocus, to emphasize and become practitioners of what they had forgotten. Others believe that it can "jump start the confidence" of those who have lost their way and need the passion and fire the movie ignites in the viewer.

Others appreciate the movie's emphasis on feeling. The joy and abundance of life are exaggerated by visual and kinesthetic effects, which is a real treat for those who learn by sight and feeling. This is not a boring lecture, a dry textbook, a judgmental sermon, or an academic treatise.

By far, most people deeply appreciated the emphasis on positive thinking and gratitude. We are taught to "look for the blessings" and "take responsibility for how we see things".

Others simply point out that putting The Secret into practice has changed their lives. It saved a marriage as the positive hope in the DVD led a couple to "bounce right back from negativity by realizing how futile it is". Others found that it sped up their growth like an elevator ride through life.

One five star reviewer puts it this way:

"I saw this movie in a private screening today and thought back to my life over the last year or so. I was always a pessimist and very hateful and bitter, despite being very blessed, and finally got tired of seeing my (young) life be followed by a black cloud. I took the very difficult step to remove negative 'friends' from my life and take action. Fast forward 2 years and I am living my dream-self employed running my dream event/wedding planning business, getting out of debt, and love myself!"

He goes on to say:

"This movie is yet another step in this process for me and I know it was no accident that I very recently met the friend who hosted the movie screening. Whether or not you believe in fate, blessings, Law of Attraction or whatever-this movie will inspire you."

A final theme emphasized by those who are pro-Secret is that it made them more deliberate as they went about their lives. We are invited to be a "deliberate attractor".

Many people were exuberant about the change that The Secret has made for them. One person went so far as to say that it "puts every self-help book to shame". Others described it as if it were magic:

"Life-changing events started taking place in my life" as soon as The Secret was unveiled.

The largest reason people are pro The Secret is that they feel supported by the mysterious cosmic force that is sending blessings their way.

We live in an age that can explain away anything. At no point in this book do we want to "explain" things away. After all, most of us want a little mystery and magic to remain in life. And we want a sense of wonder, which has been pecked away at by scientists, philosophers, cynics, psychologists, neurologists, and a host of people who pull back the curtain on our Wizard of Oz world.

It is easy to see why people like, and even love, The Secret.

It is "positive," gratitude inducing, a lively reminder, and most importantly, it resonates with feeling—feelings of joy, hope and possibility and self-regard.

Most of all, its overall message is the vast, wonderful cosmic message that the Universe is on your side.

This message is delivered with total confidence and certainty.

And all this makes a lot of people feel really good.

And so it has a receptive audience because the public loves hope, optimism, simplicity, and a short cut.

This does not mean that everything about The Secret is accurate or spiritually on target or philosophically astute.

But is it not magnificent, and often the case, that even the things people disagree over often bring about good results?

And so it is sweet that The Secret saved a marriage and that the world will hear a message advocating gratitude and possibility and abundance.

It beats whining, despair and negativity in most opinion polls.

THE OTHER SIDE

Nevertheless, a lot of people vehemently disagree with The Secret.

The most frequent complaint, made even by its advocates, is that The Secret is no secret and that it has all been said before with greater emphasis on effort and little about self-induced genocide.

Many reviewers cite the earlier works of Wallace Wattles, Napoleon Hill, James Allen, Ernest Homes, and Norman Vincent Peale. Others prefer the more modern authors of positive outlook like Wayne Dyer, John Ruiz, or Tony Robbins.

Some find it full of "easy answers" with "gaping holes in logic" and the "tiniest amount of factual support". Many viewed the film as a moneymaking scheme for the writers and that the writers themselves are not the experts they claim to be. They are viewed as "self-appointed visionaries".

Others argue that there is no "how to" in the instructions and that it is actually "pseudo- scientific babbling" that does not go deeper than an infomercial.

Still others regret what is missing in the film: there is no teaching about our inner resistance, and little if no emphasis on action or helping others.

Various speakers on the DVD say that many viewers will be shocked by the concept that we attract everything in our lives. The speakers admit that it is hard to understand but basically say nothing other than that. Of course, this is where the critics go to town in the most vehement way, as you can tell from the following two excerpts from Amazon reviewers:

"By far the most offensive part of the message is the suggestion that people who have pain in their lives are somehow attracting it with their thoughts. Darfur rape victims did not ask for it. Children who are molested did not ask for it. Starving Africans did not ask for it. To suggest that their 'incorrect thinking' is the cause of this is sickening. Positive thoughts may help you endure pain, and help you find meaning in it, but it will not end random violence, illness and war. Shame on anyone who tells a sick person that they are manifesting it themselves, that they don't want to get well badly enough."

Another reviewer says this:

"If we believe what 'The Secret' tells us, then children in African nations who are kidnapped and turned into child soldiers or sex slaves only have their own negative thoughts to blame. Farmers in Bangladesh whose food and homes are destroyed in floods are creating this themselves. I believe that this sort of thinking is sick and twisted. It allows grotesquely rich individuals to say, 'I am rich thanks to my thinking - you have exactly the same opportunity as me, therefore I should feel no obligation to help those who are less well off'.

It also seems to say that because 'the universe will provide', we can all have exactly what we want. This seems shockingly shortsighted given the growing consensus that if we don't slow our consumption of the earth's resources, there won't be a habitable earth in a few generations time. So anyone who really wants it badly enough can have a $4M mansion. Why is it that these people all seem to want more and bigger and better STUFF? That's why I say this is about greed."

As you can tell from the above review, as each person evaluates The Secret based on their our own system of values.

The Secret may be shallow, as some say, but we come from our depths to our unique conclusions

The reviews reinforce the notion that in yet another area we can divide the world in two—those who are pro Secret and those who are against it. It is a very hot issue—people seem to be strongly for or against. There are not many nominal and mild reviews on this website.

What came through very clearly in the 839 reviews, given that the average review is 4.5 out of 5, is that for many, many people The Secret is a refreshing, motivational, inspirational, positive reinforcement. It delivers an "I can" message that makes people aware of their potential. It helps people see what they are capable of.

Some people candidly pointed out that, whatever the flaws of The Secret, it is better than "ghetto law" or all the movies that are banal and all the people making money on death and destruction.

As the weeks have rolled by, there were less people complaining about the blaming of the victims in The Secret philosophy—though the ones that did were quite vehement in their wrath.

As we will examine later, there were quite a few places where reviewers offered readers what logicians call a false dichotomy. For example, the alternative given in a lot of reviews is that you are either a resigned victim of circumstance or everything is your creation. Likewise, some people think you are either all pro-Secret or you are for negativity. In truth, one can be at times a victim of circumstance and at other times in control of an outcome.

And one can be partially in favor of something and partially against it.

However, the discussion surrounding The Secret is not mainly one of logic.

As marketing experts tell us, people buy something or don't buy something based on emotion and passion. This is certainly clear from Amazon.com.

Here is the most startling impression from reading all these reviews. Some people are so transformed by The Secret that it is as if they are on the one coast of the United States applauding and cheering and yelling out their approval. And some people are so annoyed with The Secret that it is as if they are on the other coast booing and complaining and deriding the central viewpoints and consequences of The Secret. And given that they are 3,000 miles apart the audiences can't hear one another.

It is this contrast and position that makes a discussion about The Secret so compelling. In many ways, this book is an explanation of the distance between viewpoints and all that goes into the 3,000 mile difference.

Chapter Three
So What's The Problem With The Secret?
(BW)

"Everything we shut our eyes to, everything we run away from, everything we deny, denigrate, or despise, serves to defeat us in the end." - Henry Miller

The Secret promises to teach us how to use the Law of Attraction to get anything we want out of life. In the movie, we see the Universe granting wish after wish.

From shiny new bicycles and jewelry to sports cars and mansions, we are assured that nothing is beyond our reach if we petition the universe just right.

In this sense, The Secret comes across as little more than another get-rich-quick promise, albeit on steroids. Though the book and DVD of The Secret are relatively inexpensive, if we wish to learn more about these ideas by studying under some of the teachers involved, we better be prepared to pony up big time.

Of course, the prices, descriptions and structure of their workshops and services change from time to time so it can be difficult to determine exactly *how* much of an investment might be required. However, as of this writing, if one were to study under James Ray, just one of the many teachers in The Secret, it could run into the tens of thousands of dollars. Here are just some of the courses along with their current prices that James Ray offers on his website:

Creating Absolute Wealth	$3,495
Quantum Leap	$3,495
Modern Magick	$5,695
Practical Mysticism	$5,695
Spiritual Warrior	$7,695

Now remember, this is despite the fact that we are told The Secret DVD contains **"ALL the resources you will ever need to understand and live The Secret."**

In other words, we've already been given The Secret, which will give us everything we want in life. What more could I want than everything?

And if The Secret stopped here, with just the promise of material riches, perhaps it would not have drawn the degree of criticism it has. Sure, some people may be left with broken dreams and heavy debt, but that is something we seem to have grown used to today.

But The Secret *doesn't* stop with the promise of material riches. Not by a long shot. According to their official website, www.thesecret.tv:

"This is The Secret to everything - the secret to unlimited joy, health, money, relationships, love, youth: everything you have ever wanted."

In the film Reverend Michael Beckwith tells us, "I've seen kidneys regenerated. I've seen cancer dissolved."

We hear from one woman who says she cured her breast cancer in just three months by watching funny movies on TV and visualizing herself as being healthy. She also informs us she did this *without* radiation or chemotherapy.

Not only are we told that The Secret is the key to everything we have ever wanted, we are also told that it works every time:

"When you think of the things that you want, and you focus on them with all of your intention, the Law of Attraction will give you what you want, every time." Rhonda Byrne, The Secret

Though these claims may seem extreme, they are not much different than the types of claims we might hear in some religious circles. But unlike religion, we are told the Law of Attraction works independent of one's faith or belief, that it only responds to our thoughts, not our desires:

"The Law of Attraction doesn't care whether you perceive something to be good or bad or whether you don't want it or whether you do want it, it is responding to your thoughts." – Bob Doyle

And just in case there is any remaining doubt about the truth of their claims, we are told that they are verified by scientific research:

"...there is more than enough evidence, scientific evidence at a quantum physics level or physics level and neuroscience level to suggest this (the Law of Attraction) is true." John Assaraf on Larry King Live, March 8, 2007

Larry King: "Is this science, Joe?"

Joe Vitale: "It sure is on a fundamental level whatever you focus on you get more of...It's absolutely workable, testable science."

And it is here that The Secret crosses the line and acquires the potential to do harm to many who place their trust in it. When we couple claims of scientific validity with the extreme promises being made, The Secret can no longer be seen as harmless hype.

The fact is, not everyone turning to The Secret is looking for a quick buck and a fast car.

According to the March 19, 2007 issue of People magazine, a New York woman recently signed a $15,000 contract to have her house painted despite not having the money to pay for it. As a true believer in The Secret, her reasoning shouldn't be surprising. She says, "I have no idea where the money is going to come from, but there is no question in my mind it will all work out."

On the March 26, 2007 episode of her show, Oprah Winfrey backed off of her once enthusiastic support of the film for this very reason. After her shows on The Secret, Oprah received a letter from a woman who had been diagnosed with cancer and, despite being told by three doctors she would need to have a mastectomy, she decided to heal herself. Why? Because of what she learned from The Secret and seeing Oprah's shows about it.

Not surprisingly, Oprah clarified her position, saying in part, ***"What I believe about the Law of Attraction, I want to clarify it. I want to say it's a tool. It is not the answer to everything."***

Exactly…just a little late.

The sad fact is there are well-meaning, desperate people who are putting their trust in this film and those who support it. And these people deserve to know the truth about the ideas they are gambling the rest of their lives on.

"If we have a wish – a desire – and another person has the ability to deceive us the way a magician deceives an audience, we may wrongly believe that he has the ability to fulfill our wish. And the result may be comic, serious, or even tragic." Nathaniel

Schiffman, Abracadabra – *Secret Methods Magicians & Others Use to Deceive Their Audience*

The Trouble with Feelings

If our thoughts could really create our reality, then it would behoove us to become aware of them and quickly.

While we may never know exactly how many thoughts we have each day, 60,000 seems to be the most commonly used estimate. But whether or not that estimate is accurate, there is no doubt that the actual number is awfully high. So trying to monitor each thought wouldn't just be difficult; it would be impossible.

Why? Because for every thought you were able to successfully monitor, you would automatically create a new one. In this case, you would create a thought about your monitored thought. Of course, at some point you'll need to monitor this *new* thought to determine if *it* is positive or negative, if it makes you feel good or bad, etc. So for every thought you would be able to monitor, you'd just add another one to your "to do" list.

Of course these meta-thoughts might simply push some of the original 60,000 thoughts out of the way to make room, but still, monitoring our thoughts would be a daunting, if not pointless, task.

Even those involved in The Secret realize this. And as a result they encourage us to resist the temptation to monitor our every thought and instead use what they call our "Emotional Guidance System" to guide our behavior:

"Your emotions, your Emotional Guidance System, is what helps you to understand what you're thinking." (Esther Hicks, *The Secret*)

"The emotions are this incredible gift to let us know what we're attracting." (Bob Doyle, *The Secret*)

Given that we undoubtedly have fewer feelings each day than we do thoughts, using an Emotional Guidance System seems to be a more reasonable alternative. However, there is one major problem with this approach; it may not work much better.

While the nature and usefulness of our feelings may not be an issue within the narrow confines of the self-help community, it *is* an ongoing issue among psychologists. In fact, there is real debate among psychologists about just how much control we can exert over our emotions, how aware we are of them, and how accurately we even understand them.

In his book, *Strangers to Ourselves – Discovering the Adaptive Unconscious*, Dr. Timothy Wilson tell us,

"Affective reactions such as evaluations, moods, and emotions may be the specialty of the house of consciousness…however, the story is not so simple. Feelings are often conscious, but they can also reside elsewhere in the mental neighborhood."

And this "residence" is what Dr. Wilson refers to as the adaptive unconscious.

Citing numerous studies and examples, he makes a compelling case that while most of us may have a pretty good understanding of our own feelings, it is anything but a given.

Dr. Wilson points out three situations in which we may be unaware of our feelings.

First, something inside us may repress them from our awareness, as they would be too disturbing for us to consider. Second, we may simply fail to notice that our feelings have changed until after the fact. And third, our own conscious theories about our feelings may lead us astray.

Though he concedes these situations are probably the exception, he states, "The conditions under which people fail to recognize a feeling are probably not all that rare."

And if we wrongly believe that we are fully aware of, and can trust our interpretation of, our feelings, and then base our decisions upon them, we may be in for some unpleasant surprises.

In her book, *A Mind of Its Own – How Your Brain Distorts and Deceives,* Dr. Cordelia Fine discusses how important it can be to be able to use our emotions in our decision-making, but she also points out that it can be detrimental:

"…using emotions as information brings its own peril – the danger of mistaking the cause of those emotions. If we misattribute our emotion to the wrong source, thinking it stems from some origin other than the one that is actually causing our surge of feeling, this error can be carried forward to our judgments and decisions. Research suggests this may happen rather more often than we realize."

So while simplifying our emotional life by describing it as an Emotional Guidance System may be appealing, it may not be very effective. But the notion that we are not fully aware of our feelings is not the only problem with this system. Even if we were fully aware of our feelings, there is still some debate about how much control we can even exert over them.

Dr. David K. Reynolds, in his book *Constructive Living*, offers a number of principles in regards to our feelings. The first is:

"Feelings are uncontrollable directly by the will."

Though he does admit we can exert some influence on our feelings indirectly, he cautions us to remember, "…we can't think ourselves into a constant state of bliss."

But what harm could there be in trying?

Maybe not much.

But then again, maybe quite a bit.

In certain situations and with certain individuals, the desire and subsequent attempt to control our own emotional lives just might exacerbate the problem.

According to Dr. Daniel Wegner, Professor of Psychology at Harvard University and author of *White Bears and Other Unwanted Thoughts:*

"When we cannot change our realities, we turn to our minds and hope that we can control what goes on there from the inside. But this control is a swindler, a charlatan that runs off with our minds and gives us nothing in return. The suppression we crave does not save us, and instead can energize the obsession we wish to avoid."

This possibility may be one of the reasons Dr. Reynolds offers the following as his second principle: **"Feelings must be recognized and accepted as they are."**

The Trouble with Black and White Thinking

"There are only two emotions from our perspective. One feels good and one feels bad." - Esther Hicks

Throughout The Secret we are encouraged to view the world in a polarized, black and white fashion, for example:

People, events, and circumstances can be judged as either positive or negative. Feelings can be evaluated as being either good or bad. Our actions can be seen as being either inspired or uninspired. We should focus on things we want and not on things we don't want.

We are then encouraged to use these types of evaluations to help us decide upon the actions we will take in our lives.

"Our feelings are a feedback mechanism to us about whether we're on track or not. Whether we're on course or off course." - Jack Canfield

[Ed. Note. Canfield's statement is scientifically inaccurate.]

"It's really so simple. 'What am I attracting right now?' Well, how do you feel? 'I feel good.' Well good, keep doing that." - Bob Doyle

Though the simplicity of this type of thinking may be very appealing, as with the notion of an Emotional Guidance System, it can lead us to make some very bad decisions.

First, many things in life can feel bad, yet be good for us.

Physical therapy. Chemotherapy. Vigorous exercise. Intense studying. Fasting. Sexual abstinence. Staying on a budget when you would rather spend freely. Etc.

Second, many things in life can feel good, yet be bad for us.

Unprotected sex. Drinking alcohol. Taking drugs. Smoking. Overeating. Eating fatty foods. Spending freely. Seeking revenge. Etc.

Third, many situations in life simply do not lend themselves to being categorized as being positive or negative, good or bad.

For example, imagine your doctor informs you that your cholesterol level is higher than he or she would like it to be.

Is this information positive or negative?

We can't answer that without taking into account a number of other factors.

What scale is the doctor using to make the recommendation? Perhaps your doctor is simply being overly cautious and there is really nothing to worry about. Thus, this information isn't positive or negative; it just is.

Imagine that you use this information as motivation to begin a diet and exercise program you have been meaning to start for some time. Wouldn't this decision turn what might otherwise have been seen as a negative fact and turn it into a positive one?

The point is, **we cannot simply take circumstances and feelings in and of themselves and determine whether they are good or bad.** Part of this is due to the nature of the circumstances and part is due to the decisions we make because of them.

Let's take a more complex example. Your boss asks you to relocate to another city and assume a new position within your company.

Is this positive or negative?

Again, there is simply no way of knowing without weighing other factors.

Would you be making more money?

Would you be taking on additional responsibility?

If so, are you willing to accept more responsibility or would you be happier staying in your present position? What about your new coworkers or neighbors? How would they compare to those you have now? How might your family be affected by such a move?

The number of considerations is essentially endless and as a result you may not be able to say beyond any doubt whether such an event is positive or negative.

How about circumstances that are clearly positive or negative such as getting fired or finding out you have cancer?

Even these may not be as black and white as we may think.

For example, Seven-time Tour de France winner Lance Armstrong has often talked of how he decided to use living with cancer as a source of motivation to achieve even greater things.

As for getting fired, most people would probably agree that that is a bad thing.

However, bestselling author Harvey Mackay found 28 people who might disagree with that assertion and he wrote about them in his book, *Fired Up!: How the Best of the Best Survived and Thrived After Getting the Boot.*

In sharing stories of such notables as football coaches Lou Holtz and Bill Belichick, NYC mayor Michael Bloomberg, actor Robert Redford, and talk show host Larry King among others, Mackay clearly shows us that even being fired isn't as black or white as it may seem.

How can we make decisions based on whether or not things are good or bad when our decisions themselves often determine whether things are good or bad?

Black and white thinking also tends to destroy diversity and tolerance in our lives by encouraging us to only associate with like-minded people:

"Learn to become still and take your attention away from what you don't want, and place your attention on what you wish to experience." – *The Secret*

"And when you see those things that you are not wanting in your experience, do not talk about them. Don't write about them. Don't join groups that worry about them. Don't push against them. Do your best to ignore them." – Esther Hicks, *The Secret*

It is easy to see how reading these quotes might lead people to simply avoid hearing from people who disagree with, or otherwise do not support them. In other words, "negative" people. And yet, diversity and tolerance are essential to everyday life.

Nobel Peace Prize recipient John Hume said, "Difference is of the essence of humanity. Difference is an accident of birth and it should therefore never be the source of hatred or conflict. The answer to difference is to respect it. Therein lies a most fundamental principle of peace: respect for diversity."

And the philosopher Voltaire once said, "What is tolerance? It is the consequence of humanity. We are all formed of frailty and error; let us pardon reciprocally each other's folly. That is the first law of nature."

Diversity and tolerance are difficult qualities to embody when we simply turn our heads away from those with whom we disagree.

Encouraging people to see the world in black and white terms may also lead some people to avoid the most effective solutions to their problems.

Remember the woman who claims to have cured her own breast cancer by watching funny movies and visualizing herself being healthy?

Whether or not this type of approach may be effective in fighting cancer, if a person believes it might be from watching The Secret, that person might be tempted to try it at the expense of treatment with a proven track record.

Why might a viewer make such a potentially harmful decision?

Several reasons.

For one, we are told the Law of Attraction is supposedly a universal law that works every time, all the time. If that is true, what possible risk could there be in relying on it alone?

We are also assured that the Law of Attraction is based on science. Since medicine is also based on science, doesn't this imply parity between the two healing methods?

And finally, we are told that simply thinking and talking about things can cause them to manifest, even if we don't want them to come true.

If believed, this puts us in a real bind. Consider...

Esther Hicks tells us in the original version of *The Secret*, "**And when you see those things that you are not wanting in your experience,** do not talk about them. Don't write about them.

45

Don't join groups that worry about them. Don't push against them. **Do your best to ignore them**."

But John Demartini tells us that every form of healing has a place. The question is, how can one follow the advice of both Esther Hicks and Dr. Demartini?

Since traditional medical treatment *requires* us to speak with physicians about our medical problems, and *forces* us to think about our medical problems each time we take medicine or receive treatment, isn't this simply "reaffirming" the existence of our medical problems? If so, isn't this going against the advice offered in The Secret?

People may say this is a ridiculous conclusion for people to make. But why is it so ridiculous? If people are being told by "authorities" that the Law of Attraction is a scientific fact that works every time, no exceptions, and they believe what they're being told, why wouldn't they make such a conclusion?

Apparently some in the medical community think it could happen as well and that the results could be tragic.

"If you think that you're not going to get cancer, you don't want to get cancer, you believe you're not going to get cancer, are you not going to get a mammography, are you not going to have a colonoscopy, are you not going to quit smoking?" Professor Richard Sloan, Columbia University Medical Center, ABC World News Tonight, March 16, 2007

"If someone follows this book literally, that would guide them to not taking the preventative steps they need, or if they are diagnosed with cancer. If some person chose to strictly follow the steps in this book there is a risk they could die needlessly." Dr. Richard Wender, President of the American Cancer Society, Nightline, March 23, 2007

Law of Attraction and the Coming Guilt You Will Feel

Several tenants of the Law of Attraction geared toward the acceptance of personal responsibility can be particularly harmful despite how empowering and innocuous they may first seem.

First is the idea that we are 100% responsible for everything that happens in our lives.

According to The Secret:

"You are the only one who creates your reality. For no one else can think for you. No one else can do it. It is only you. Every bit of it you."
"EVERYTHING in your life you have attracted. Accept that fact. It's true."

Second, we are assured that the Law of Attraction works every time.

"The Law of Attraction is really obedient," says Lisa Nichols, one of the teachers in The Secret. "When you think of things that you want, and you focus on them with all your intention, **the Law of Attraction will give you what you want, every time."**

And finally, we are assured that the Law of Attraction is easy to practice.

"This is like having the universe as your catalog and you flip through it and you go, 'Well, I'd like to have this experience, and I'd like to have that product and I'd like to have a person like that.' It is you just placing your order with the universe. It is really just that easy." – Joe Vitale

But what happens if we accept responsibility for everything in our lives and it turns out we *aren't* responsible for everything?

What happens if it turns out the Law of Attraction isn't quite so obedient and doesn't work every time?

And what happens if getting what we want using the Law of Attraction isn't as easy as just placing an order with the Universe?

What happens is that a darker side of The Secret becomes readily apparent as guilt quietly moves in and takes the place of hope.

While the notion that we are 100% responsible for everything that happens in our lives may sound empowering, and perhaps can even *be* empowering at times, it simply doesn't hold true as a universal principle.

Many factors come into play in determining how we behave, and few of them are within our everyday awareness and as a result even fewer are under our conscious control.

Numerous psychological experiments have demonstrated just how easily certain aspects of our social environments can dramatically affect our behavior. Here are just two examples:

Stanley Milgram's experiments (as documented in his book "Obedience to Authority") tell how he used the presence of authority to induce average people to willingly administer what they thought were potentially fatal shocks to innocent people.

And Philip Zimbardo's infamous Stanford Prison Experiment, in which college students acted out the roles of either prisoners or prison guards, led to such volatile behavior and psychological breakdowns that the experiment had to be stopped before it could even be completed.

Both of these experiments demonstrate the situation Eric Hoffer described in his book called *The Passionate State of Mind*:

"The people we meet are the playwrights and stage managers of our lives: they cast us in a role, and we play it whether we will or not. It is not so much the example of others we imitate as the reflection of ourselves in their eyes and the echo of ourselves in their words."

And aside from the impact others have on our behavior, the mere presence of certain words and images can have an enormous impact on our behavior without our being aware of it. Psychologists refer to this as "priming" and it has been well established for years.

Granted, these are just some of the outside factors that can affect our behavior, not to mention other obvious ones such as our genetics, the conditions into which we are born and raised, and our personal experiences.

By suggesting that we are 100% responsible for the circumstances of our lives, The Secret leads us to overlook the degree to which these other factors come into play. As a result, our lack of awareness of these factors can make us *less* capable of compensating for them. And this can lead to a downward spiral that can be difficult to escape.

After all, if we mistakenly believe we are responsible for certain circumstances in our lives – such as disease, poverty, violence, abuse, etc. – and we are unable to correct our circumstances by "correcting" our thoughts, who else is to blame?

And according to The Secret, the guilt we will feel is well founded because our thoughts are, in fact, the cause of our disease:

"Our physiology creates disease to give us feedback, to let us know we have an imbalanced perspective, or we're not being loving and grateful." – John Demartini, Chiropractor

"Disease cannot live in a body that's in a healthy emotional state." - Bob Proctor, Public Speaker

And unfortunately, by focusing all our attention on correcting our own thoughts and feelings, we may overlook solutions that might otherwise help.

According to Dr. Edward M. Hallowell, a psychiatrist and author of Worry – *Hope and Help for a Common Condition*, when patients accept what Dr. Hallowell calls a "guilt-laden self-diagnosis," **they may think there is something wrong with themselves, thus producing shame on top of guilt. And as a result, "If they feel ashamed, they cover up their symptoms as best they can and deny themselves the very help they need, help that could change their lives."**

And not only would we be missing out on the help we need, we would be fighting a battle that virtually guarantees our defeat:

"One can try to recreate the world, to build in its stead another world in which its most unbearable features are eliminated and replaced by others that are in conformity with one's own wishes. But whoever, in desperate defiance, sets out upon this path to happiness will, as a rule, obtain nothing. Reality is too strong for him. He becomes a madman who, for the most part, finds no one to help him in carrying through his delusion." – Sigmund Freud, *Civilization and its Discontents*

What about the value of hard work and struggle?

"Action will sometimes be required, but if you're really doing it in line with what the universe is trying to deliver, it's going to feel joyous, you're going to feel so alive, time will just stop, you could do it all day." – Bob Doyle

Notice he said "sometimes."

In other words, at other times action *won't* be required. The universe alone will respond to your thoughts alone and bring you what you want. Of course, we see numerous examples of this in the film itself.

In one scene, a young woman is shown admiring a necklace through a jewelry store window. In the next scene, the necklace is magically around her neck.

In another scene, a young boy appears to get a new bike just by obsessing about it. He doesn't get a paper route, a job at a fast foot restaurant, or even mow a few lawns to earn the money. He simply thinks about the bike, looks at pictures of the bike, and before you know it, it shows up on his doorstep.

While the "easy way through life" may sound great to many of us, to see how the promise of riches without work can be harmful, we need only ask ourselves one question:

Is this how we want our children to approach the problems in their lives?

Do we want them to sit around wishing and dreaming about things? Or, do we want them to set goals, make plans to achieve them, and then go out and take the action necessary to achieve them?

By avoiding those things that stress us, that may confuse us and cause us discomfort, we may deny ourselves the opportunity to experience true breakthroughs in our lives.

Thomas Edison, one of the historical figures who reportedly knew "the Secret" once said, "Opportunity is missed by most people because it is dressed in overalls and looks like work."

How does this square with the idea that work isn't always necessary and in those situations where it is necessary, it should be joyful and effortless?

Perhaps Edison knew a different secret after all...

What about the needs of others?

But perhaps the most disturbing side effect of The Secret is that by encouraging us to focus on our own desires, we overlook the needs of others.

Though many who love The Secret may disagree, we only need to listen to the words of the producer of the film, Rhonda Byrne, to realize just how self-absorbed this philosophy is.

In what appears to be her last interview before dropping out of sight, Rhonda Byrne told Oprah Winfrey, **"If you see people who are overweight, do not observe them, but immediately switch your mind to the picture of you in your perfect body and feel it."**

So if we don't want to be overweight, we shouldn't look at people who are. Of course, given that "we bring about what we think about," we should also avoid the poor, the hungry and the sick.

And though this strategy may do wonders for the practitioner's state of mind, it does nothing for those who need our help the most. After all, if we cannot look at them, it won't be long before we forget about them.

In the end, it appears the message of The Secret is not all positive and empowering. It is also selfish and destructive. And those who embrace it stand to lose far more than they may gain.

"Many persons have a wrong idea of what constitutes true happiness. It is not attained through self-gratification but through fidelity to a worthy purpose." Helen Keller

Chapter Four
The Law of Attraction
(BW)

Is it really a "Law?"

Is it something that even works once in awhile?

It sounds powerful. It sounds official. And from what we're told by those involved in The Secret, it is. For example:

"When you think of the things that you want, and you focus on them with all of your intention, the Law of Attraction will give you what you want, every time." (Rhonda Byrne, *The Secret*)

"What you think and what you feel and what manifests is always a match, every single time. No exceptions." (Esther Hicks, *The Secret*)

"We have an absolutely unlimited power within us and it's really an exciting time...because it's a time when spiritual positions and science are now in total agreement." (James Ray on *Oprah*, February 8, 2007)

"...there is more than enough evidence, scientific evidence at a quantum physics level or physics level and neuroscience level to suggest this (the Law of Attraction) is true." (John Assaraf on *Larry King Live*, March 8, 2007)

Those are some strong words. The Law of Attraction works every time, no exceptions, and they have the scientific evidence to back it up.

Or do they?

In an earlier segment of the same *Larry King Live* episode just referenced, John Assaraf said,

"We know that we are made up of energy and we know that we can actually measure a thought, we can measure the frequency by which our brain and our heart sends out that frequency. We are just learning more about the scientific side of it. *We don't have triple blind studies to really show that.*" (Emphasis added)

So they don't have the studies to show that the Law of Attraction *is* true. But they say they have enough evidence to *suggest* that it is true. **The fact is there is no evidence in the field of quantum physics to suggest anything like The Law of Attraction is real.** None. Nada. Zip.

There isn't a sober scientist on the planet that would ever say such a thing. It's like saying that your couch can fly.

References to scientific evidence and the specter of quantum physics give the Law of Attraction a certain mystique that suggests it is beyond the understanding of most people. But as we are about to see, this is not the case. In fact, since the Law of Attraction is supposedly "always working" in all levels of our lives, it should be relatively simple for anyone to determine if the claims being made on its behalf are true. And in this chapter we'll do just that.

As we're about to see, we don't need to be quantum physicists to demonstrate that the Law of Attraction, as taught in The Secret, isn't scientific, that it isn't a universal law, and that it isn't necessarily an effective strategy for getting what we want out of life. In fact, we might just discover that it never works.

Is the Law of Attraction as presented in *The Secret* scientific?

According to some involved with The Secret, there is no doubt that the Law of Attraction is scientifically sound. The following exchange is from *Larry King Live* on March 8, 2007:

Larry King: "Is this science, Joe?"

Joe Vitale: "It sure is on a fundamental level whatever you focus on you get more of. If you're focusing on lack, you're going to get more lack. If you focus on abundance, you're going to get more abundance."

Joe Vitale: "I tell people find something in your life right now to be grateful for because at that point you will start to attract more things to be grateful for. *It's absolutely workable, testable science.*" (Emphasis added)

Joe Vitale is someone with an obvious interest in metaphysics, one of the teachers featured in The Secret, and one of its most vocal supporters.

But when ABC's Cynthia McFadden asked Columbia University physicist Brian Greene about a similar question, she received a very different opinion. While Dr. Greene acknowledges that there is a Law of Attraction, he says it doesn't support the claims being made in The Secret.

Cynthia McFadden: "Can one use the Law of Attraction, as you understand what it means, to gain wealth, to gain success, to get thin, to cure cancer?"

Dr. Greene: "I know of no way to use the Law of Attraction as we've talked about it in physics, gravitational attraction or electro-magnetic attraction, to directly through the power of thought cause anything in the world around us to happen one way or another." (*Nightline*, March 23, 2007)

This seems to directly contradict Vitale's position. Of course, one could assume that this contradiction may simply be the result of Dr. Greene not being as familiar with The Secret as Vitale. If so, then perhaps another physicist who is more familiar with The Secret would support Vitale's position. But according to *Newsweek* magazine, this is not the case.

An article in the February 25, 2007 issue of the magazine says *both* quantum physicists who are featured in the movie – John Hagelin and Fred Alan Wolfe – have "distanced" themselves from the idea that we can get the physical universe to fulfill our wishes solely by wishing.

One of them, Fred Alan Wolf, is quoted as saying, "I don't think it works that way. It hasn't worked that way in my life."

Now remember, these are two quantum physicists who actually appeared in The Secret. Given their knowledge, their experience and apparent openness to the ideas in the film, wouldn't it be safe to assume that if any quantum physicists would support the scientific validity of these ideas, it would be Wolf and Hagelin?

And yet, even they do not appear to fully support the claims made in the film.

Again, there is an enormous difference between "evidence that proves" and "evidence that might suggest." And it just might be the difference between The Secret being a "New Era for Humankind" - as is suggested on their website - and just being more New Age nonsense.

And as it stands, it's getting easier to see exactly where on this spectrum The Secret falls. Given the lack of conclusive evidence showing the Law of Attraction to EVER WORK, in ANY CIRCUMSTANCES, everything starts to fall apart around The Secret.

No evidence.
No studies.
None.

The claim that The Secret is a "New Era for Humankind" seems premature, at best, doesn't it? But does a lack of conclusive proof mean that it is New Age nonsense? Not necessarily. It could simply mean that tests haven't been conducted yet. But even if this were the case, there is still a major problem with trying to test it: it isn't clear exactly what we would be testing.

According to the film, in a very basic form, the Law of Attraction says that at the level of thought, like attracts like.

How does this work?

We are told that thoughts have frequencies that can be measured and that we emit these frequencies constantly. In other words, our minds may be thought of as powerful transmitters, which transmit the current frequencies of our thoughts. These thoughts are then, "drawing the parallel back" to us from the Universe.

And we are assured that, "It always works. It works every time, with every person."

This sounds like it would be a simple thing to test. We think about something and see if we attract it into our lives. If we do, that supports the Law of Attraction. If we don't, that disproves the Law of Attraction because according to the film it always works, every time, with every person. As a result, it only takes one failure to prove that it does not work as promised.

It's pretty simple.

But as The Secret progresses, we learn that the Law of Attraction isn't quite so clear-cut. It seems there are some apparent disputes about how to actually invoke this law.

Some teachers assure us it responds solely to our thoughts, whether or not we actually want our thoughts to come true. Another tells us we must also focus on our thoughts with all of our intention. Others stress that how we feel about our thoughts is also an important factor. And while one teacher assures us that action may "sometimes" be necessary, another tells us we must have our thoughts, feelings *and* actions all in alignment in order to invoke the Law of Attraction. We are also told that it is always working whether we believe it or not. *Then* we are told that we must ask, *believe* and receive. And finally, we are told that there is also a time-delay involved so no one can say for sure how long it will take any given thought to manifest.

At this point, it becomes impossible to test the Law of Attraction. It becomes impossible because there are so many subjective factors involved (e.g. thoughts, beliefs, intentions, actions, feelings, etc.) that an apparent failure of the law can be explained away in numerous ways. For example:

"We weren't thinking clearly enough."

"We weren't feeling strongly enough."

"We didn't imagine our goals in enough detail."

"We didn't take enough action, or we didn't take the right action."

"We didn't really believe we could attract it."

"We had an unconscious counter-intention."

"We haven't allowed enough time to pass for the Universe to respond."

In other words, either we didn't "apply the law correctly" or we didn't *really* want what we thought we wanted, so the universe, in its infinite wisdom, chose not to grant what we thought we wanted, but simply matched whatever frequency of thought we were emitting. Thus, "proving" once again the Law of Attraction does in fact work every time, for every one, no exceptions.

Notice how the Law of Attraction compares to the law of gravity, which says something like, if you hold up a rock and then let it go, it will fall to the ground.

Period. That is something we can test and all agree upon the results we obtain.

Of course, if the law of gravity said that if you hold up a rock and *think* it will fall, and you focus on it with all of your *intention*, then let it go, the law of gravity will make it so, every time, we'd be in the same predicament we are in with the Law of Attraction.

Even if it were true that we didn't think clearly enough, feel strongly enough or whatever, how could we ever know this was the case? There is no way we can measure the clarity of our thinking, the strength of our feeling, the completeness of our imagination or determine if we've allowed enough time to pass. To say that these explain the apparent failure of the experiment and thus prove the validity of the Law of Attraction is wishful thinking.

In his book *The Demon Haunted World*, Carl Sagan tells a story called The Dragon In My Garage, which also features a flawed hypothesis. During a fictional dialogue in which a skeptic is unable to disprove Sagan's claim that he has a dragon in his garage, Sagan explains:

"Claims that cannot be tested, assertions immune to disproof are veridically worthless, whatever value they may have in inspiring us or in exciting our sense of wonder."

They are not only veridically worthless, that is, useless in helping us determine the truth, they are also not scientific.

"Such explanations are said to be nonfalsifiable. Their falsity cannot be determined by any conceivable test. For an explanation to be scientific, it must be falsifiable." – Charles M. Wynn and Arthur W. Wiggins, *Quantum Leaps in the Wrong Direction*

So at this point, without ever performing a calculation or taking a single course in quantum physics, we can see that the Law of Attraction – as presented in *The Secret* – is, by definition, not scientific. Some may say that this isn't a fair statement because their version of the Law of Attraction seems to be validated by some aspects of quantum physics. But to take aspects of a sub-atomic theory and try to apply them to *all* levels of our daily lives is again, wishful thinking.

What happens between two particles at a sub-atomic level may have little or nothing to do with what happens between two people in a social setting. As a result, at this time, the Law of Attraction should take its place amongst other metaphysical ideas and be treated accordingly.

Is the Law of Attraction a Universal Law?

Just because this version of the Law of Attraction doesn't meet the scientific criteria at this point doesn't necessarily mean that there isn't something to it. Perhaps one day it will be validated as a scientific theory and truly usher in a "New Era of Humankind" as promised on their website. Of course, if this ever happens it would mean that the Law of Attraction is, in fact, working this very moment. That would mean we should be able to observe it and determine if it behaves as we have been told it does. If so, how might we determine this?

Well, one teacher in The Secret, Mike Dooley, tells us that, "...these laws of the universe - some would call it quantum physics - are as predictable as gravity."

Another teacher, John Demartini, assures us that, "If you look very carefully, when it comes to The Secret and the power of our mind, the power of our intention in our daily lives, it is all around us. All we've got to do is open our eyes and look."

So, if the Law of Attraction is as predictable as gravity, and all we have to do to see it is to open our ideas and look, let's do just that and see what kind of evidence we might be able to find.

While The Secret offers numerous examples in support of its claims, our job is to see if we can disprove them. (By the way, that's what science is all about. It's not being unkind or "negative." It's the job of a scientist to try and prove the Law of Gravity as accurate or inaccurate-- so we truly know, one way or the other).

If we can't, that provides more evidence in favor of the Law of Attraction. But if we can find just a single case that proves it doesn't work as we've been told it does, that would cast serious doubt on the claim that it is as predictable as the law of gravity.

As we consider the following examples, remember that according to The Secret, the Law of Attraction works "every single time, no exceptions."

Alcoholics Anonymous and Other Twelve Step Programs

Alcoholics Anonymous has been helping people overcome their addiction to alcohol since the mid 1930s. Though it is anything but a guaranteed approach to the problem, it is certainly the most enduring and has been responsible for helping countless alcoholics successfully battle their addictions.

Though AA and other programs based on AA use a twelve-step model, three of them are particularly interesting given our investigation into The Secret.

The first step in AA is to admit one is powerless over alcohol and that his or her life has become unmanageable.

The fourth step is to make a thorough and fearless moral inventory of oneself.

The fifth step is to admit the exact nature of our wrongs to God, to oneself and to another human being.

Now contrast these with the notions we've been taught in The Secret.

Rather than admitting we are powerless over alcohol and that our lives have become unmanageable, we are to imagine ourselves to be powerful and in control of our lives. In fact, to do otherwise would make our recovery less likely and our lives less manageable – every time, no exceptions. And yet, it doesn't.

Rather than making a moral inventory of ourselves, we should instead just focus on our positive qualities. To do otherwise would be to manifest more of our moral defects – every time, no exceptions. And yet, it doesn't.

And finally, rather than admitting our wrongs openly, we are not to talk of them.

"And when you see those things that you are not wanting in your experience, do not talk about them. Don't write about them. Don't join groups that worry about them. Don't push against them. Do your best to ignore them." (Esther Hicks, *The Secret*)

In fact, we shouldn't even join groups like AA because they *do* talk about alcoholism and we don't want more of that in our lives. To allow ourselves to be in a situation like this is just inviting more alcohol addiction into our lives – every time, no exceptions. And yet, it doesn't.

Granted, AA does not work for everyone, but it does work for many people and its success has spawned many other recovery programs. Of course, if the Law of Attraction is truly a universal law, AA shouldn't work for anyone, ever. No exceptions.

Exposure Therapy and Paradoxical Therapy

Exposure Therapy is a type of psychotherapy that aims to cure people of phobias by repeatedly exposing them to the very things they are afraid of until they become desensitized to them.

For example, a person who is afraid of spiders might start out watching spiders on television until they can do this without discomfort. Then, they might be asked to watch spiders in an aquarium that is placed across the room until they once again can do it without discomfort. They are to repeat this over time, getting ever closer to the spiders until they reach a point where they can actually hold a spider without fear. While not effective for everyone, exposure therapy can be very effective for many people.

A recent television program featured a young woman who was afraid of flying. A therapist instructed her to repeat the words, "The plane is going to crash," to herself hundreds of times a day until the words no longer frightened her. Then, he had her do the same with the phrase, "I want the plane to crash."

The result? Though she didn't attract a plane crash, she did lose her fear of flying.

A similar type of therapy that is even more extreme is known as Paradoxical Therapy. When using Paradoxical Therapy a therapist may instruct a patient to intentionally engage in behavior that he, the patient, wants to stop. For example, if a patient suffers from obsessive worry, the therapist might instruct him to set aside a certain amount of time each day to do nothing *but* worry. The interesting thing is, for many patients, this actually helps them gain control over what was initially an uncontrollable behavior.

Now contrast these types of therapies with the notions we've been taught in The Secret.

Rather than exposing a client to thoughts and objects that are troublesome for the patient, the therapist would instruct the patient not to think of, nor get anywhere near, these things. Instead, the patient would be instructed to think of something they would rather have in their lives. To do otherwise would only exacerbate the problem, every time, no exceptions. But it doesn't.

And rather than instructing a patient to intentionally engage in unwanted behavior, the therapist would instruct him to avoid it at all costs. He'd also tell him not to think about it or discuss it with anyone. To do otherwise would simply make matters worse – every time, no exceptions. And yet, it doesn't.

Medical Research

Every day across the world medical researchers study diseases and other medical conditions in an effort to find cures and/or better treatments for these conditions. Past breakthroughs from this type of research have been so significant that our average lifespan has nearly doubled in the last hundred years.

And since there appear to be no reports to the contrary, these researchers must not be experiencing any higher rates of these conditions than the average population does.

If the Law of Attraction is a universal law that works every time, no exceptions, how can this be? Think about it.

Many of these researchers spend every day of their working lives thinking about little else *but* these conditions. Imagine spending every day studying and researching cancer, AIDS, multiple sclerosis, and countless other conditions, all the while knowing that you are attracting these very things into your own life.

Is this an absurd notion? Absolutely. But only when one examines the Law of Attraction outside the pretty box The Secret has placed it in and compares it with real life situations such as these.

Actors

Some actors are known for the extremes to which they'll go to truly master a role. It is common for them to immerse themselves in the lives of the characters they are to play for months at a time to get it "just right." And this goes well beyond physical attributes. They learn to think the thoughts their characters would think. They learn to feel the feelings their characters would feel. And finally, they begin to act as if they were the character.

Some of the characters portrayed are just average people with average lives. Some of them are good people who find themselves victims of violence or disease. And some of these characters are out to *victimize* others.

But if the Law of Attraction is a universal law, aren't these actors putting themselves in extreme danger? Given the intensity with which they prepare for a role, wouldn't they be attracting the very conditions they are portraying?

Given the "incredible power" our feelings have according to the Law of Attraction, actors should be far more vulnerable to attracting many of these unwanted conditions into their lives. And yet, they aren't.

Stalkers

If the key to attracting what you want in life is to focus on it intensely, think about it constantly, visualize yourself as already having it and to take action whenever one feels inspired, then why do stalkers rarely get what they want?

Isn't this exactly how stalkers come about? Isn't this exactly the process they employ?

They become obsessed with someone and can't think of anything else. They fantasize about this person and eventually feel inspired to approach them. And yet, they end up in jail more often than they end up with the object of their desire.

How can that be? Perhaps they didn't want it bad enough. Or perhaps they didn't fantasize deeply enough. Or perhaps they didn't act on every impulse that made them feel good.

Or maybe, the Law of Attraction isn't a universal law after all.

Some may say the above examples are ridiculous because these people (with the exception of stalkers) never actually intended to attract these things; they were just doing their jobs. But according to the Law of Attraction, this shouldn't make any difference.

Consider these quotes from the film:

"The Law of Attraction *doesn't care* whether you perceive something to be good or bad or whether you don't want it or whether you do want it, it is responding to your *thoughts*." Bob Doyle emphasis added)

"Most people have a goal of getting out of debt. That will keep you in debt forever. Whatever you are thinking about you will attract. You'll say, but it's get out of debt. *I don't care if it is get out or get in. If you're thinking debt, you're attracting debt.*" Bob Proctor (emphasis added)

So the notion that cancer researchers aren't *trying* to get cancer shouldn't matter. The fact is, they are thinking about cancer almost constantly. And yet, it would appear they don't have any greater chance of getting cancer than the general population does.

The idea that actors are just pretending and not trying to actually attract the types of characteristics they portray shouldn't matter. They not only think about these characteristics, they try to feel them deeply and then they act upon these as if they were true, so that they can create the most believable characters. And according to James Ray, one of those featured in The Secret, this combination of thoughts, feelings and actions should guarantee the Law of Attraction would come into play:

"...you've got to go three for three. You've got to have your thoughts, your feelings and your actions all firing and in alignment.

"And what I would say to our caller is that there's probably one of those components missing. You look at anybody who's not creating what they desire and deserve, and they're missing one of those components. You've got to go three for three.

"And when you do that, you've really creating the life you deserve." - James Ray on *Larry King Live*, March 8, 2007

Three for three. Isn't that just what actors are doing?

The one element we really haven't touched on in these examples is belief.

The Power of Belief?

According to some teachers in The Secret, belief that we will attract our desires is essential. But are there situations in which even *this* powerful strategy could fail to attract those things we focus on? Let's find out.

Hypochondriacs

A hypochondriac clearly thinks about illness. In fact, that may be virtually all he thinks or talks about. He also acts as if he is sick with the illness he imagines himself to have. Because of this obsession, he even begins to feel the symptoms of his imaginary illness. But to him, the illness is not imaginary. He is convinced he is sick. That is, he believes he is sick. And while he may have a mental illness, he rarely has the physical illness that lives only in his mind. Despite his thoughts, feelings, beliefs and actions all "firing and in alignment," he fails to attract the disease he obsesses about into his life.

Even if the hypochondriac tries to attract a disease as common as cancer, he is unlikely to have much luck.

"There is no evidence that people attract cancer by their thoughts."
Dr. Richard Wender, President of the American Cancer Society,
Nightline, March 23, 2007

It is probably a safe bet that the same could be said of diseases
such as AIDS, heart disease, tuberculosis and possibly even a virus
such as the common cold. Though if our thoughts were as
powerful as The Secret tells us they are, we would constantly be in
danger of attracting these and many other diseases at every turn.

There is no doubt we could find many other examples from our
everyday lives that would directly contradict the Law of Attraction.
And yet, true believers will continue to defend the idea and offer a
myriad of excuses and distinctions that appear to defend the
validity of their beliefs.

What is particularly interesting is that once we take into account
these excuses and distinctions in order for the Law of Attraction to
make sense, it suddenly seems like plain old common sense:

In order to get what we want, we must clearly know what we want,
have a burning desire to get it, believe that we can get it, be willing
to do whatever it takes to get it and have patience along the way.

Does this sound like a "universal law" to you? Does this sound
like an idea that history's elite would have been desperate to keep
away from the masses? Does this even remotely sound like a
secret to anyone?

At this point we know that the Law of Attraction isn't scientific
and we know that it isn't a universal law on par with gravity.

But still, even though the Law of Attraction doesn't work as well
as The Secret would have us believe, it could be argued that it *is*

one of the best strategies we have for getting what we want out of life. Unfortunately, even this isn't always the case.

When the Law of Attraction Sets Us Back

"When you are visualizing, when you have that picture playing out in your mind, always and only, dwell upon the end result." Mike Dooley *The Secret*

"You provide the feelings of having it now and the universe will respond." *The Secret*

The Secret tells us that visualization is important. It also tells us that we shouldn't visualize anything except for the end result we are trying to achieve. In the movie we see a man sitting in his living room visualizing what it would be like to have a brand new sports car. It is realistic, it is thrilling and, unfortunately, it just might be the worst way to actually try to attract that car.

According to Daniel Gilbert, a professor of psychology at Harvard University,

"...thinking about the future can be so pleasurable that sometimes we'd rather think about it than get there." Then later, he describes a study in which volunteers "were asked to imagine themselves requesting a date with a person on whom they had a major crush, and those who had the most elaborate and delicious fantasies about approaching their heartthrob were *least* likely to do so over the next few months." Daniel Gilbert, *Stumbling on Happiness* (emphasis in original)

If visualizing in great detail with strong emotion is the key to getting what we want, and it works every time, no exceptions, how come the people mentioned in this study are exceptions?

Perhaps Joe Vitale can offer some insight. In The Secret, he tells us, "This is such a holographic experience. So real, so real in this moment, that you don't even feel like you need the car because it feels like you already have it."

Then, if we no longer feel we need to attract our goal, perhaps we will no longer be willing to work for our goal. If so, wouldn't it make sense that some people would be content to simply enjoy the feeling and skip the work involved entirely?

Remember, The Secret tells us, "You provide the feelings of having it now and the universe will respond." It seems that if we apply this approach, we'd better hope the universe will respond, because we may not.

At this point, some people may think, "So what if the Law of Attraction isn't scientific? So what if it isn't a universal law or even if it isn't always the best strategy for getting what we want out of life? It clearly helps some people so where is the harm in teaching these ideas?"

And these people do have a point; these ideas *do* seem to help some people. However, what they are forgetting is that these ideas may be hurting other people at the same time.

Chapter Five
The Truth Behind the Lie
(KH)

The Secret is an encapsulization of a recurring wish for magic to be real.

Shoot, everyone wants to be able to play Quidditch. We all have hoped for potions and spells to be effective at rendering a teacher or professor silent for a day...we all want to be able to fight off evil detractors...

It's the simple notion that you can blink your eyes or wiggle your nose and that which you desire will appear....that Santa Claus really will come down the chimney...(and if anyone wanted to believe that...it would be me) ...the simple notion that these things are real is where things start to get unsettling...and for most people on this planet, offensive.

And I should be precise. The philosophy is not about Santa Claus or wiggling your nose. Specifically I am most concerned about an ideology that comes from higher beings in the universe channeled through a human who then teaches it to a bunch of people as a "law of the universe" like gravity.

This chapter refers specifically to Byrne's contribution to her own book. Some of the contributors gave useful content (Denis Waitley, for example). But Ms. Byrne is living in a disconcerting non-reality.

The Magical "Law of Attraction"

The premise of the measurable part of the philosophy is the "Law of Attraction." The idea is that if you can mentally attract it, it will come. "It's just as easy to attract $10,000 as it is $1," the author says.

(I can't measure spirit beings channeling info to people.)

"Attract a feather...it will come."

Not if there are no birds on your island, it won't....

Unfortunately, there is either an unkind lie or a big mistake happening.

Obviously if you live in a free country you can control much of your destiny IF you are physically able and in reasonably OK above the neck....and attributing your level of success to the Law of Attraction or God or your kids is fine. BUT, when you take that attribution and bring it to people who don't live in the richest nation(s) on earth we painfully see that the "law" doesn't apply....

But here's the thing:

God doesn't withhold the money from the people of the African continent because they are unable to "believe enough", nor does he bless the Americans (or Australians) because they believe so much better.

The "Law of Attraction" as it is presented in metaphysical literature like The Secret is indeed an untruth and a mistake.

To simply point out someone else's error and leave a void would be pointless. Before I continue with discussing the serious problems that lie within The Secret, let's find out what DOES work.

The Attraction Principle

The Attraction Principle, on the other hand, is rock solid science. The Attraction Principle is about "priming." It's a complex reality inside the brain, but it's fairly simple in principle: If you "filter" for something, you're more likely to see it.

I introduced *The Attraction Principle* in 2002.... after reading and testing the Law of Attraction as it was incarnated 5 years ago.

The Attraction Principle is a principle I developed into a process that seems like a metaphysical concept, when in reality it is a principle grounded in science. The Attraction Principle helps you use Covert Hypnosis to direct your thinking (or that of someone else) so they have the tools necessary to optimize their chances of reaching their goals.

You See That Which You Already Have in Your Mind

An illustration will help start us out.

Last time I bought a car, I decided to purchase a Honda Accord. Consumer Reports said it was the best car in its class. (Even better than the Camry I once owned.) So, I simply went to the Honda dealership and asked to buy the Honda Accord. I didn't even know what a Honda Accord looked like. I just brought my checkbook and pen. They showed me a bunch of models and, ultimately, I bought a gold Accord. It rode beautifully on the test drive and I was fine with it. I wrote the check and shortly thereafter I was out the door.

As I was driving over to the office I noticed several things. The first thing I noticed was that there were a LOT of Honda Accords and quite a few that were seemingly as new as mine! Everywhere I looked on the road I saw the Honda logo and most often it was attached to the Accord. I hadn't remembered seeing an Accord in weeks before my 20-minute drive to the office. This day I saw a dozen Hondas en-route. I was really quite surprised at just how many people owned these cars!

Of course I ultimately remembered that I used to see Toyotas. I saw Toyotas everywhere for the previous ten years. I saw Avalons and Camrys and Celicas and Corollas everywhere. But now of course I owned a Honda and my reticular activating system in my brain was picking up Hondas....everywhere. My brain had a new filter and antenna. It filtered out all the other cars and brought to my attention all of those cars which were like that which I owned and now liked.

That's how the brain works.

Women know that when they buy a shirt or a dress they notice that everyone else wears the same thing! Of course no more people own the shirt or the dress today than did a few days earlier, but indeed the brain now filters out all of the unimportant stuff and filters in all of that which is "yours" or important to "you." The brain is a remarkable piece of craftsmanship.

The Difference between Success and Failure

Now, what's wonderful is that the *Attraction Principle* is just like this. Napoleon Hill figured this out 75 years ago...that focused attention and focused faith matters...and it wasn't new then. Even in old writings like the Bible there are hints on "that which you think on is yours."

Of course "manifestation" is just one of two key parts of the *Attraction Principle*. The other part is ACTION. Getting someone to take action though is a bit more challenging than simply thinking of attractive things and people they want in their lives!

Some people can get a real clear picture of what they want in their mind and they are presented opportunities everywhere to acquire that thing or state of mind but they don't take action on accomplishing or acquiring the desired object.

The *Attraction Principle* in Healing

Let me share with you how powerful the *Attraction Principle* is to me.

When I found out I had Hyperkeratosis/Leukoplakia on my right vocal cord earlier this year, I knew I had a pre-cancerous lesion and that I could be in serious trouble. I knew I had to take as much action as possible to help the Mind/Body link start whatever healing process could possibly take place.

I went to the University of Minnesota medical library and read everything I could about Hyperkeratosis and Leukoplakia. Most of what I read was very ugly. The reality of cancer was fear provoking, but I knew from my Mind Body research that the more you know about a disease or disorder the better your chance is to recover for it. I finally found the medical book that had the surgical procedure for removing the leukoplakia. I memorized the procedure. I knew that I would have to have general anesthesia, something I did NOT want to experience. I knew they would put a mouth guard on my teeth to protect it from the tube that would get inserted into my throat.

I learned how to use the laser that would be used to shave the leukoplakia off my cord and I learned how to take a biopsy...I saw it go under the microscope and I heard the lab people saying, "the cells are fine, no signs of cancer at all."

I did this operation between 20 and 50 times per day in my mind. The one- hour procedure could be done in about 5 minutes in my mind. Sometimes I did the procedure in my mind and I was fearful. Eventually it became boring and more matter of fact to where I seriously determined that I could do it on my self with a local anesthetic!

Four weeks to the day after the diagnosis I went back for a recheck. I still could hardly speak and had no volume. And, on that day, August 7, the doctor said, "It's gone."

Just like I had imaged it hundreds of times. Of course it was gone, I had done the surgery over 500 times in the four weeks. (This is what is known as a miracle...and they call them miracles because they don't happen all that often!)

But please stop here: A crucial part of thinking is to say, "Hey, Kevin, that is really great...but I noticed you went back to the doctor."

Oh yes.

The *Attraction Principle*:

If you wanted to break it down to its two most significant components it would be this...

Imaging the Process x Directed Action = Close to the Desired Result

Now, don't think that every imaging will manifest itself in real life because you think it will.

Also, don't believe for a moment that just because I took all the right actions by researching hyperkeratosis and leukoplakia that it means that everyone will get well in similar circumstances. I simply utilized the resources I had at hand and was fortunate enough to have a positive result.

Of course, this can be a chronic condition. Many people have hyperkeratosis, it's removed surgically and it comes back. I know that I also have to take other actions to make sure that doesn't happen!

For the Honda, of course there are lots of other cars out there. I still see Toyotas and other cars but I see a lot more Hondas than other cars because it is important to me.

We can help people with the Attraction Principle. We can ask people to determine who and what they want in their life and clearly image that or that person. Do they want a business partner, a boyfriend, girlfriend, spouse, money, travel to an exotic location? Whatever it is, that's the starting point. That's got to become the clarity and certainty of ownership. Just like the surgery. It has to be obvious and second nature that the result is there.

Next, you must make a mental map of specifically what they will do in order to acquire that result, person, type of person or thing. Everything starts with a thought but without action, the concept of manifestation is simply a leading cause of frustration.

Your friend must do and be prepared to offer energy, effort and value for that which they want and desire.

What follows is a blueprint for utilizing the *Attraction Principle* in a helpful manner. It is a rudimentary model that you can adapt to most people's specific needs!

81

The *Attraction Principle* Pattern

Step one: "Close your eyes and allow yourself to breathe. Focus on your breath. (Have your client take three deep breaths, in/out and put all of their attention on their breath.) There have been many things and people you have wanted in your own life…for some time…and now…I would like you to focus your attention and intention on just one very specific thing or person or kind of person you want to appear in your life….now…when you have this in mind raise your right finger."

Step 2: "Now what I want you to do is tell me, in great detail, an experience where you have this person or place in mind."

(They describe this to you.)

Step 3: "Excellent. Now, I want you to tell me, in great detail, another time (place) where this person/thing is in your life…in the very near future…"

(They describe this to you.)

Step 4: "Excellent. Now, I want you to tell me, in great detail, another time (place) where this person/thing is in your life…in the very near future…"

(They describe this to you.)

Step 5: "Now what I want you to do is tell me all of the specific steps and the sequence of steps it will take fulfill this manifestation into your life."

(They should give you a detailed process. If they don't prompt with and after you ask: " what happens next?" "And then what".

THE PROCESS THEY DESCRIBE TO YOU SHOULD BE AN
OBVIOUS SEQUENCING THAT OPTIMIZES THEIR
DREAM/PERSON/GOAL/RESULT/OUTCOME.

Step 6: "Excellent. Now, in great detail, describe for me why you
must allow this person/thing to come into your life beginning
now."

(They describe this to you.)

Step 7: "Wonderful. Now, bring the picture of this
person/place/thing clearly into your mind in such a way that it is
very enticing and makes you excited and energized." –pause-

(OR whatever emotions are appropriate to this specific
person/place/thing!)

"...allow yourself to experience this now and see all of the
enjoyment, excitement (again be appropriate to the context of the
desire) and happiness this will bring you and tell me when will you
begin the process of bringing this into your life?"

Step 8: "Very good. Now, pay attention to your breathing and
when I say the number one, you can open your eyes and feel
energized ready to bring in to your life all that you richly deserve.
3...2...1..."

So, if I tell you to be aware (or not be aware) of dogs this week, I
promise you will notice dogs....far more often than you will have
dreamed possible. Dogs.

If you say that you want to earn $100,000 next year on the Internet,
it's pretty easy to make that happen. The Attraction Principle goes
to work in the brain.

The importance of the Attraction Principle is that our primed awareness IS relevant to our achievement and success in life. In fact, it's paramount to both.

However, it is by no means a *law*.

I only could wish that were true....

Imagine...If I'm in Somalia, I can "attract" all the food, water, and AIDS vaccines I "believe in", and I will die right next to the other million children.

That is where the Attraction Principle (that I've written about for a decade) is so fundamental. If there is no food in the environment or possibility it will come, the brain still filters for it, it just isn't "findable" because it is not there.

You won't believe this but **one promoter of The Secret wrote and told me that if the Africans had faith, they would have food.**

In fact, I would challenge the promoters and authors of The Secret, promoters of the so-called "Law of Attraction", to hop a bus or train or plane to Somalia, with stops in other famine-ridden, war torn locations in Africa and see just how unattractive the purported "Law of Attraction" is.

Were that it could be true.

But this is one of the greatest deceptions.

So the promoters sit next to the dying child in Somalia and say, "no, no, no believe harder." "Do it."

And she closes her eyes and dies.

84

She couldn't believe well enough, efficiently enough, hard enough....

Insane.

That child like all children doesn't know what reality is.

Children believe what we tell them.

And they die right next to the adults who believed the purveyors of deadly guilt.

And they ALL deserve to LIVE.

Well, the author and promoters of the "Law of Attraction" come to the conclusion that the BILLION people that are in Africa have earned the right to starve to death, as they do not believe. They refused to accept the $10,000 as readily as the $1.

If you believe in a God, is that really what you believe?

If you believe there is a connectedness in the universe and that we are all connected is THAT REALLY what you believe....that the person who is a part of you gets to die of starvation because they didn't read The Secret??

But the Law of Attractioner....doesn't... feel guilt, because, of course, according to their guess, the Africans have attracted the life they were meant to have. Past life, a lesson, something they must learn.

Thank God the author has a limo.

Thank God the promoters have private jets.

And let's propose that the Law of Attractioners fly over to China on the jets.

Smoggy and bustling cities. Impoverished in the rural. Another BILLION people. 500 million of which will rot away...

The "Law of Attractioners" come to the village but because the 500 million can't believe enough or effectively enough, they all rot away as well...

Back to the private jets and this time off to Cuba where the poverty isn't as bad as Africa. These people have shacks at least, and, typically, water. Millions of them.

The "Law of Attractioners" have lunch on the jet before landing because there is no good food to attract.

They spend the day teaching the impoverished Cubans how to use "the Force" like Yoda, but the Cubans are apparently as "stupid" as the Africans and Chinese were. These damn non-English speaking people...

No attraction today. No $10,000. No $1. Nothing.

They mutter to themselves, "We've used this law for years back in America and we've gotten all these jets and everything. Why can't these people simply apply the law? It works for us!! That's how we know it's a law!!!"

Back to the plane.

Off to California where people have the decency to speak English. A stop at my little friend James' house in Clovis.

James is a real life Kindergarten-age kid that isn't going to Kindergarten.

Because of a stroke he suffered as an infant, he can barely move his body. Barely smile. Thanks to stem cell therapy he can do those two things. He'll get a couple of more treatments, but the "Law of Attractioners" have to tell his parents that this is what they have "attracted into your life."

The little boy is destined, fated to have this life.

But to heck with the fact the little boy can't talk beyond a couple of drooling words.

That's his destiny.

How about the $10,000 here?

Sorry family, Mom has to stay home all day to take care of the boy. There will be no $10,000 attracted every month for 5 years for treatments.

The "Law of Attractioners" teach the family how to attract. They hold their Yoda-like hands out, close their eyes and believe. They are convinced...they are faithful...they are positive...

...but nothing comes.

...only more pain and tears.

The "Law of Attractioners" tell them they have attracted this life. It's their destiny. They didn't believe right...much like the Africans, the Chinese, Cubans...

Except all of them did believe. They bought into the story and now have been left to die with guilt instead of simply starving to death, had the "Law of Attractioners" left with them alone on their way out of the country.

Ah...and then we go to dinner with the "Law of Attractioners"...perhaps in Hollywood where the book is selling very well indeed...where people believe and receive....

They order dinner but it never comes because the kids in the back are all manifesting away...believing that they will not need to work tonight and will certainly have the money on the table in the morning...and will have no need to do something as hard as save for college....the school work doesn't need to be studied because attracting $10,000 is as easy as $1 and they apply the simple law to their homework.

Except... they fail the test. They end up on the street because they believed a little too much and did a little too little...

...and no dinner was served.

...but it doesn't matter...it wasn't meant to be... Irritated, the Attractioners depart and are happy to hop in the limo and go home to a delightful gourmet dinner that they attracted last week, cooked because they thought it (and because a servant cooked it.)

...they fall asleep thankful...being blessed that they believed...in the "Law of Attraction" and knowing that for the billions of others they taught, it simply wasn't meant to be. Those that starve, that die of dysentery...it doesn't matter because it was their destiny. All is as it is supposed to be as they turn over and fall asleep...as they have an afternoon taping of the next TV show where they will go and harm and permanently scar another million lives with the belief in the magical "Law of Attraction".....................

Chapter Six
Digging Deeper into The Law of Attraction
(KH)

If you don't want to get fat, Rhonda Byrne, author of The Secret, offers this advice: "If you see people who are overweight, do not observe them, but immediately switch your mind to the picture of you in your perfect body and feel it."

Is this naive or deplorable?

Replace the word, "overweight" with a different word, like "handicapped," "people with Cerebral Palsy," "people with Muscular Dystrophy," "people dying of AIDS," "people who are paralyzed," "people who are homeless," "people who are starving."

See the problem?

The great teacher's philosophy is if it is ugly, look away; if it feels good, do it; if you don't want it, don't look at it.

People have said, I should, "just try it."

Huh?

Why?

I want to become a sociopath like that Law of Attractioner?

No thanks, I'll use the ATTRACTION PRINCIPLE that I developed about 2002 and take advantage of how the brain works to achieve success.

When people can simply LOOK AWAY from the child with cancer or the burn victim so they can "feel good inside," I'm sorry, that's a bunch of first class crap. That is horrifying to me. I don't want to "try" anything that has this level of cruelty no matter how much chocolate syrup someone puts on it.

And you think I exaggerate the horror of her teaching?

Byrne goes this far and FURTHER.

Here is her response to a question about the women and children being raped and butchered in Rwanda:

"If we are in fear, if we're feeling in our lives that we're victims and feeling powerless, then we are on a frequency of attracting those things to us ... totally unconsciously, totally innocently, totally all of those words that are so important."

Yup, she's saying it's the women and children's fault.

So, ladies, the Law of Attractioner advocates are obligated and would have you believe that if you have been raped, it's your fault anyway. You deserved it because that was the result you got.

Insane logic?

A friend of mine attracted a speeding ticket the other day because he was speeding.

The Attractioner works from result to premise.

You got it, therefore, you asked for it.

Same for children that are molested.

Same for those who starve.

Oh yeah, that's making me feel real good inside. Nice warm fuzzy.

It's become almost a religious cult fad that has an obvious viral effect. Lessons to be learned for all marketers here....

But WAIT

Serious Problems with "The Law"

There is another problem and this one is even MORE SERIOUS.

People can attract genocide as easily as they can a new BMW. They can attract a feather even if there is no bird.

Shoot.

This is a LAW of SCIENCE (according to Attractioners).

We are so in trouble....

If so, then there is nothing to "believe in."

IT is going to "WORK" whether you like it or not.

Like gravity.

Nothing to believe in or "try."

It just WORKS.

Except when it doesn't of course...which is...always.

It wouldn't draw my ire except that it causes pain on the individual and societal level and strips people of their hard earned money.

Marketing Lessons Learned

Marketers....James Cameron, the movie producer has caught onto this and has now indicated he believes that the bones of the family of Jesus have been found. And millions will believe and go see his movie. I'd explain why those bones almost certainly are not from Jesus or his family but space permits only one topic at this time.

Marketers...a lot of people never put their brain in gear. You read the story about Mother Mary in the pizza pan...an obvious miracle...a sign...proof of God...

I mean after all you know what Mary the Mother of Jesus looked like right? You know she uh....wait...they didn't have cameras back then and Jews didn't draw or paint images of people as it was an abomination to their God. Oops. Well IF we knew what she looked like, trust me she'd look like the lady in the pizza pan.

Now, let's just pretend that that was a PHOTOGRAPH in the pizza pan and there have been cameras for two millenia....

What are the odds it would be the Mother of Jesus?

Why would it be the Mother of Jesus?

Why wouldn't it be your Mom or Mine????

It has to do with a "Secret" called Priming....

Priming and the Brain

As soon as you give people what is called a "Prime", they are influenced to believe whatever that Prime was and will think in "contexts" related to the prime.

If I say George Washington...then ask you to write down the name of a man, most people write down the name of a historical figure in American History....like Thomas Jefferson or Ben Franklin.

If I say Jesus, Christians tend to write one-word names like, Paul, John, Mark, Matthew, Thomas.

That's one kind of priming.

Is the photograph in the pizza pan Mary the Mother of Jesus?

Obviously not, but millions will tell you it is, because it "looks just like her," except we haven't a clue what she looked like. Not a clue in the world. But we are primed by the thought of having TV, cell phones that take pictures, you name it....and never remember that there were no images of people in those days painted or drawn by Jews.

And are they the bones of Jesus' family?

Why Jesus the son of Joseph and Mary, and not one of thousands of other families? The probability is so tiny it's barely worth looking at. (And yes they should look and check it out).

Now you take all this DaVinci-esque cool stuff and pop it on the cover of THE SECRET and you are primed to BELIEVE.

To say this is brilliant marketing is to fall short. It is beyond brilliant. Byrne, this TV producer with no thought or care for humanity and the human condition certainly can make a quality production. She understands how mainstream women think. She has captured it brilliantly.

And the marketers out there hawking the book did a great job. Just about the best promo I've ever seen.

93

But really, I am thankful that The Secret is a Lie, The Secret isn't anything close to a physical law like gravity.......

.... because if it were true, I would have the ability to cause people's death just by thinking about it...worse...they could cause mine....or I could cure people just by thinking about it...or worse...they could give me some horrible disease by using their thoughts to manipulate the physical universe....

Which of course is one step short of insanity...or every plane that went up would crash and every person with a fear of heights would fall to their death.

Those with a fear of spiders or snakes would attract thousands of them to theatrical terror.

Now STOP.

Can simply dwelling on something bring it to fruition?

Can Simply Dwelling on Something Bring it to Fruition?

You think I'm being sarcastic but that is what Rhonda Byrne says happens when you live in fear of something. That's why all the poor Rwandan women and children were butchered, murdered....remember?

And if people stop looking at you, realize it's because people who have THE SECRET don't want to look at fat people. That's how you lose weight.

I kid you not. Rhonda Byrne SAID that in the same interview she explained how the children of Rwanda brought on their own genocide. (Not the fault of the killers, the fault of the CHILDREN.)

94

From *Newsweek*: "The Secret" is saying: Its explicit claim is that you can manipulate objective physical reality—the numbers in a lottery drawing, the actions of other people who may not even know you exist—through your thoughts and feelings.

In the words of "author and personal empowerment advocate" Lisa Nichols:

"When you think of the things you want, and you focus on them with all of your intention, then the Law of Attraction will give you exactly what you want, every time."

Every time! Byrne emphasizes that this is a law inherent in "the universe," an inexhaustible storehouse of goodies from which you can command whatever you desire from the comfort of your own living room by following three simple steps: Ask, Believe, Receive.

Thankfully, no one, has that kind of power or ability....nor would want it.

Chapter Seven
Understanding the Secret Law of Attraction
(KH)

Oh how I wanted to believe the "Law of Attraction" was "real." It was 1994 and I wrote, *Life By Design*, the only book I ever had to put "out of print". Too many of the principles and ideas in the book were like the "Law of Attraction" and as the evidence came in, it was obvious that my desire to believe was far greater than what was happening in the real world.

So, we deleted the book. It was frustrating. Being able to believe in the universe as something that we have a significant impact on through the quantum field was a pretty cool notion. And of course there was a lot more to it than that, but it was flat out incorrect.

It would be very easy to sell out and write persuasive pieces supporting "The Secret" and get on Oprah.

It's an easy sale for Oprah's demographic.

I'd quintuple my income over night.

From a money-only perspective, I'm crazy not to do so.

But as much as I enjoy having a full wallet, a full heart is important, too. An honest character doesn't hurt any, either...so I have "attracted," (chosen) to be flat out direct about "The Secret" and the "The Law of Attraction."

What's another 20 million....

If you want to skip ahead to the provocative stuff toward the middle of this chapter, I don't blame you. If you can handle a little bit of background....hang in there with me.

Creating and Attracting Success

I want success. You want success. However we define it.

I've spent 20 years creating a life and attracting the people I want into my life. I'm pretty happy with my results.

Now, notice I said, "creating" and "attracting." There is everything right and nothing wrong with "attracting" good stuff into your life. There is everything right and nothing wrong with "attracting" good people into your life....even a car (though you do get a payment book with the car, so that one is a bit of a fairytale).

You and I both MUST do everything we can to create our best environment and world to live in. We should do everything we can to attract a safe and nurturing environment filled with gratitude. Without exception.

One thing I've been grateful for is the 8-year relationship I've had with readers of the e-zine *Coffee with Kevin Hogan*. I've got one of the highest IQ demographics for readership on this planet. *Coffee with Kevin Hogan* readers all dress better and speak more articulately than I do. And that's whom I attract. I don't attract idiots. Thank God....

People Move Away From Fear

People consistently seek out situations where they will be comfortable (with individually predictable exceptions). People don't want to fear, don't want to experience pain....and if someone gives us an easy and super-quick, "fix," boy is that attractive!

Don't a lot of people think, "If I can pay just about anything to keep me comfortable and in the money...I'm there...?"

People Want "It" Now

The fact is you and I want food at the moment we want it. We get irritable waiting in line at the drive through. If we wait four minutes, we wonder what is "taking so long". We want sex when we want it, at least I do...We want sleep when we want it. We want acceptance. We want inclusion....someone says we can have all that just by thinking...shoot...that's not a bad deal...

And we don't want to have to "pay" for the food, the sex, the sleep, the acceptance, the inclusion. But there is a price for all. Some people try and bypass the price and steal the food, the sex, the sleep, etc. Others try and pay the least possible price. Still others pay full price....

Part of the problem is this interesting word, "work". It's a four letter word for most people...oh wait...it is four letters...well you know what I mean...Most people in the United States work pretty long hours compared to the rest of the world. We put in about 40-45 hours per week. Europeans freak out when you approach those hours...and most "successful" people put in about 60 hours per week.

People who hate 40 hours of "work" each week sure as heck don't want to hear about 60 hours of work to have any kind of a great life. Screw that. They'll take "balance" instead.

What doesn't show up in the stats or on the list of secrets...is that successful people generally are doing something they enjoy, are challenged by or have passion for....and that is a HUGE SECRET.

Successful people don't want to work 80 hours per week at something they hate! In fact they don't. Successful people

99

(measured by life satisfaction, standard of living, etc.) simply like what they do. McCartney recently told an audience, "Why would I retire, I LOVE my work."

Selling Easy

Here's a Secret...they don't want you to know...

...I know that if I make something sound easy, that more people are open to taking action on acquiring that piece of knowledge...that secret...and that is SMART on the individual's part. It makes no sense to acquire information, knowledge, wisdom that doesn't make life more efficient...better...sooner...

Clearly I can show someone the necessary steps/elements/factors in becoming a millionaire, for example. It's not difficult. Not at all.

Here's another Secret most gurus won't tell you: Human nature is not pro-millionaire. Nothing in our DNA drives people to collect pieces of paper with dead Presidents on them. Nothing in our genes tells us to save for a rainy day. Squirrels yes...humans no...Nothing.

For example...Saving for a rainy day is learned and defies our nature as people.

If I have to "save" something, that means I can't "use it" today. That means, no instant gratification and a VERY UNHAPPY HUMAN.

As a Person of Influence, just SAYING that word "save" is like cutting your income in half!

If I tell you that I can show you how to develop the mind frame of a millionaire but it requires bypassing instant gratification, you are

LESS LIKELY to take action. Not because you don't want to, but because you don't LIKE TO.

...so the guru shows you there is nothing up their sleeve and that there is no effort involved...or maybe they call it inspired action which sounds about as challenging as going to Church.

Think about this...We all want to lose weight. We just don't LIKE TO do it.

Make sense?

What we want to do is the genesis. It's the idea. The acorn...the decision to succeed...

...Most people are great starters...and don't finish what they start because of the Want/Like Paradox. Gurus don't want you to know about this. They are going to be upset that I told you, but that's life...

Human Nature Resonates With the Here and Now

What we LIKE to do is eat, play, have sex, watch TV...there is NOTHING in human nature that is pro-success. Nothing. Every guru knows that because they watch their humans do nothing because they told them there would be nothing that they would have to do...and no one calls them on it because they would be embarrassed.....

It's our nature to sit around, get food for today, meet as many desires as we can for today and "hope" that tomorrow will be fine. And that works because there is no pain to push us to do or think otherwise.

If I tell you that you can have a BMW in your driveway and Pam Anderson in your bed and all you have to do is SIT there and meditate, BELIEVE that it will happen and you will RECEIVE (get), that's an attractive philosophical idea worth looking at.

Because it fits your nature, and mine too.

Avoid looking at fat people and you will lose weight. Beats the heck out of the South Beach Diet, being hungry and doing sit-ups.

If all I want is some quick money and you and I aren't going to know each other or live in the same country in 10 years...and I have no morals or ethics, then I tell you that you can sit, see, believe, receive. That will be $1995.

The amazing thing is that people CAN have amazing things and people in their life but there a few pieces to the puzzle that go beyond thinking and attracting. (And yes I know that "inspired action" is very important in The Secret).

Principles and Human Nature

But the fact is that some humans have evolved to where principles become important in life. There are no pure people (complete, godly). But there are some darn good people.

I want to continue to be one of those "darn good" people because it's something I believe in. Something that matters. It's so important that I give up millions of free dollars by NOT being on Oprah and Larry King, supporting "The Secret". It means it's more valuable than selling out (which means getting paid to not deliver...)

I can't do it.

...and the fact is I do fine. I'll always do fine because there is a group of people who want to do business with people they trust, that have integrity and compassion. Period.

So, I might not have the easiest proposed answer, but I find solutions that will work...and I can't sit there and tell people that you attracted the life you currently have...that the children butchered in Iraq have attracted their life...that molested children have attracted their life. It's a flat out lie. Period. Anyone who suggests otherwise that's getting paid at the end of a conversation should be sent to sea.

I believe I know how to communicate, to change a person's mind and heart...to hold onto the change. I understand at a rudimentary level how the brain and mind work. I used to think I knew a lot more than I really did. I now know that it's not as simple as I once believed. I don't mind being wrong because that means I just figured out something new. You don't evolve...you die...

One thing is for sure....I can show people how to speak, write, teach, train, organize, manage their time, build significant wealth and so on...predictably. In other words, I've taken the time to find out what works and what doesn't.

Importance of an Accurate Roadmap

That's against human nature as well. People don't want to take the time. They want the instant gratification. I can come close to giving that by giving people good maps, but even good maps lead over bumpy roads...which is exactly what the map says. People want a map that says, "no time or effort required, thinking only".

Now other gurus tell you that you don't need bumps. "The Law of Attraction works every time...all the time."

OK great...except it doesn't.

So does it bother me if you take your $1995 and waste it with that guru?

103

Only a little.

People who want to believe that Pam will be at the door when they get home and are so convinced that it's going to happen every time that they will pay $1995 flat out don't get a lot of empathy from me.

Besides I've already done those things myself....yes...I too wanted the lazy way to wealth and success. I wasted money and time on bogus promises. I was dumb.

One thing is for sure...

For sure, it is TONS easier to make a million today than it was 15 years ago (adjusted for inflation even). It doesn't take HALF the work. Not even 1/4. But it does take effort, good maps, good mentors and sound decision making...and a few other things.

But INSTANT GRATIFICATION is see it, believe it, pull the handle (that's the inspired action), it comes up 777, I open the door and there is Pam holding my million for the day.

Everyone wants that...it's not even a "bad thing" to want that to be real. It IS human nature. It's reality. It's who we are as people.

But it's not how the "universe" works.

In fact the universe doesn't "work". It just keeps getting bigger. Ah...that's for another day, let's get back to Pam...

Pam will be there for her one guy, if any and that's it no matter what you or I "manifest".

This is the great reality check.

Even Kid Rock won't be seeing Pam this week when he gets home.

Now, next to fear and greed, HOPE is the most powerful motivating tool for pretty much anything (leaving out sex and the core needs we all have). So let me HOPE that Pam will be at the door...OK?!

If I tell you, visualize it, believe it, receive it...works every time...shoot,...you gotta try that.

And you spend your $1995, and I frankly don't blame you the first time around.

2K they say Pam will be there.
No 2K definitely no Pam.

One way has HOPE.

What kind of logic is at play here?

Surprisingly, it's real logic. No kidding.

What Kind of Logic is at Play

And it's interesting to know that the teenage brain makes all decisions based on this logic, and it is indeed logic.

The teenage brain hasn't learned probability yet....and sometimes never will...

If we can have what we hope for, shoot, it's a no-brainer. You do it.

Except it doesn't work...most of the time.

HUH?

Yes, there will be ONE person that will open the door and see Pam tonight. There really will. Katie Holmes WILL see Tom Cruise (probably). But your wife won't...at least not while she's awake.

So it works for Katie Holmes, but not for you.

At least that is how it seems...why does she get to Attract and you don't??

And that's another chapter in a book and not available right now...later...

So you spend your $1995. No Pam. No Tom. No million because the map you bought...stunk. It was made up without doing the actual work of marking out the terrain.

And then you call back and say, "Hey it didn't work," and they say, "It always works, you aren't doing it right."

And of course the second half of that statement is true. You can't do it right because there is no way that map will work. (Except for Katie.)

Now we see that you can't attract Pam and Tom.....but MONEY is different than Pam and Tom.

Money is pieces of paper or, as I prefer it, gold...

Money can be acquired very rapidly if you are willing to take risks....or... money can be acquired very quickly if you are willing to break civil law.

Now, let me ask you....Just what are "The Secret" teachers teaching?

What ARE They Teaching?

Hood over head. Hand in pocket. Go to bank. Demand all the money. Leave. Probability of (attracting "it") getting away with it is greater than 50%. No kidding.

But are you OK with that?

Now if I tell you that you can have all that money and all you have to do is sit, believe, receive and cut me a check for 2K, it's the same thing.

I could choose to teach you how to rob a bank.

Or I could show you how to create a huge amount of value for people, get paid incredibly well and have a great life.... And when you EARN the money and then USE it, obviously you're simply withdrawing it from the bank. It was YOURS to start with because YOU PUT IT IN THE BANK. You aren't taking SOMEONE ELSE'S.

Get it for doing nothing? It's not likely to be yours. (And there are a few useful exceptions.)

So I could choose to rob you and teach you how to be a bank robber.

I can show you how to be of genuine value to the world.

Either way you will net a similar financial dollar figure. Either way, I get paid.

Only one way do I personally respect myself. Only one way do you respect yourself.

Fact is, that when you think of something and it becomes important to you, your brain literally finds those kinds of things in the environment.

(If it ain't there to be found, it ain't there. You can picture getting to Jupiter all you want and my friend....you ain't goin'.)

The Attraction Principle

That's a piece of what I call the Attraction Principle. It's based on neuroscience. It's part of the reason a lot of people believe in the Law of Attraction. Because their brain filtered for X but it sure seemed like X magically appeared before them. Between filtering and chaos, I can assure you there was no quanta input.

Now which SOUNDS BETTER.

See it, believe it, receive it.

See it, make a plan, create a mastermind, work your plan, persist, be resilient, stay focused, act everyday and act a LOT...and there is a VERY GOOD CHANCE you'll receive it.

Hell the first one sounds better to me too!

But it works under the proposition that the universe is a slot machine...that it pays off for some people and not others. And the universe doesn't do that. There is NOT an abundance of wealth to go around. There is enough wealth on this planet for about 9,400.00 USD per person. Do the math; it is not complicated to figure out.

That said, if you speak English and are reading this (you have a computer) you really DO have the possibility and probability if you choose to have pretty much anything you want, within logic or reason (exceptions do exist, including Pam, Tom, Angelina and Brad).

If you have a computer, you can easily be a millionaire in 5-7 years. No rocket science involved. But it isn't sit, see it, believe it, receive it either.

So for the past few weeks since "The Secret" teachers were on Oprah and I've responded, I've taken my hits from my fellow professional speaking colleagues.

And it's OK.

Because they'll need help in order to sleep tonight.

If there is karma....I pity their next time around.

Chapter Eight
Following the Money
(BW)

"Get your forms and your credit cards and get to the back of the room." - James Ray on *ABC World News Tonight*, March 16, 2007

As of this writing, according to the Simon & Shuster website, there are 3.75 million copies of the hardcover version of the book The Secret in print. There are also 400,000 copies of the audio version in print. And The Secret DVD has sold over 1.5 million copies with the majority of those being sold just in the last month.

But that's only part of the picture.

Many of the teachers featured in the film have become celebrities themselves and are now packing seminar rooms with eager students willing to pay hundreds and sometimes thousands of dollars a piece to learn more about the Law of Attraction. This is despite the fact that the DVD alone promised to give viewers, "ALL the resources you will ever need to understand and live *The Secret.*" Which begs the question, if the original movie gave us ALL the resources we would ever need, why is there a sequel in the works? What more could there be to say?

Apparently, a lot.

Many of these teachers may have graciously volunteered their time to appear in the movie, but they also are selling their own line of Law of Attraction-related products and services on the side. And

111

some of these are designed to help other people become "certified" Law of Attraction practitioners and coaches themselves. At least one of these even offers a two-tiered affiliate program to encourage even more people to get involved in selling these ideas.

So while there is much debate about the validity of The Secret, there is no doubt about the success of The Secret. A lot of people are making an awful lot of money.

But is all this success due to The Secret itself? Could the success of the project itself be a testament to the Law of Attraction? Apparently some of those involved think so.

According to the official blog for the movie, Rhonda Byrne, the film's producer, "says she used the secret to make The Secret." And John Assaraf said on *Larry King Live*, "We have actually used The Secret to build The Secret."

Though these claims may be true and may have contributed to the incredible success of the film, there are also a number of other reasons. And most of these have to do with something much more mundane than universal laws; they have to do with brilliant marketing.

Some people may find the very notion of "marketing" a supposed universal law odd. After all, did anyone market the law of gravity in order to share its importance with the world?

Certified Law of Gravity Instructor…anyone?

But with the introduction of quantum physics and the myriad of interpretations offered by people who can't spell it, the game has changed.

In the book *The Cosmic Code – Quantum Physics as the Language of Nature*, first published in 1982, Heinz R. Pagels describes the situation like this:

"What we find here is a kind of marketplace – a reality marketplace. The reality marketplace has lots of shops, each with a merchant who wants to sell us his version of physical reality. It is the *interpretation* of these experiments in terms of physical reality that is being sold." (Italics in original)

Though Pagels was almost certainly speaking of a marketplace more in metaphorical terms back in 1982, today the metaphor has become reality. And The Secret has become, by far, the biggest success the self-help marketplace has ever seen.

Still, even as its meteoric rise was becoming increasingly obvious, some dismissed it as an obvious "money-grab" that would quickly suffer a backlash from consumers.

In fact, I even satirized the entire process on my website and called it The Law of Extraction.

The Law of Extraction Revealed

I've been asked to elaborate on the Law of Extraction, which I mentioned in a recent post. Since many of you have been using the Law of Attraction trying to get this information out of me, I am, of course, powerless to say no.

But first, I must confess the Law of Extraction isn't my idea. It was revealed to me recently by a channeled spirit named Ralph while I was trying to tune into a weak radio station.

Apparently this law has been known by great hucksters throughout history and kept hidden from the masses for nearly a hundred years. Only now is this information being made available to the general public.

May it bring you the happiness and success it has brought to countless gurus past and present.

And now, as revealed to me by Ralph, here are...

The Nine Steps of the Law of Extraction

1. Promise people something they desperately want, no matter how ludicrous it may be.

For example, promise to show people - for a price, of course - how to get everything without doing anything.

2. Make the process for achieving this sound as mysterious as possible. For example, call it a mystery or maybe even a secret.

3. Legitimize your process by quoting a scientist or two. This way you can claim your process is actually "based" on science.

4. Assure people your process is foolproof. That is, anyone can do it and it will work every time all the time. Calling it a universal law is helpful in this regard.

5. Include a universal loophole so that when the process fails you can place the blame elsewhere.

For example, "The reason it didn't work is because you didn't do it right. Fortunately, there are advanced techniques that can help you."

Notice, this loophole not only deflects blame, but also creates additional revenue streams (see points 6 and 7).

6. Sell advanced techniques in the form of high-dollar, back-end products, seminars and coaching programs using a multi-level commission structure in order to maximize revenue extraction.

7. Offer high-dollar "Certification Programs" to license others to sell your process to others. Be sure to require your licensees to also pay you a sizable percentage of any future sales they may make.

8. Focus your efforts on the right target audience. As the old saying goes, you can fool some people all of the time and they are the ones you need to focus on.

9. Express gratitude at least three times a day for all the abundance the Law of Extraction is bringing into your life.

Remember, the Law of Extraction is based on the principle that hope attracts money. Take pride in knowing that you are not only creating abundance for yourself, but also doing well by your fellow man.

Though the Law of Extraction was meant as mere satire, in many respects, it wasn't far off the mark. However, the expected backlash from consumers never came. Instead, as we know, The Secret book and DVD have sold in the millions with no end in sight.

The question is, why?

The success of The Secret has largely been attributed to a brilliantly executed viral marketing strategy. Joe Vitale, one of the teachers in the film and a veteran marketer in his own right, said, "I think the marketing campaign behind 'The Secret' is going to go down in history as the greatest case study of viral marketing ever done. Anywhere." – ABC News, November 26, 2006

According to Wikipedia, "Viral marketing and viral advertising refer to marketing techniques that seek to exploit pre-existing social networks to produce exponential increases in brand awareness, through viral processes similar to the spread of an epidemic. It is word-of-mouth delivered and enhanced online; it harnesses the network effect of the Internet and can be very useful in reaching a large number of people rapidly."

The concept of viral marketing seems simple enough. However, it is one thing to be able to understand it, it is quite another to be able to make it work. And to make it work to the degree The Secret has may be unheard of.

But to understand what made The Secret such an excellent candidate for viral marketing, we must explore it from a number of different perspectives. And as the picture becomes clearer, the reasons for its success will become obvious.

To begin, we will explore four different marketing aspects of The Secret: the product, the brand, the marketers and the market. We will then compare The Secret to another self-help phenomenon from the late 1970s and early 1980s called the est Training. Though the est Training did not enjoy the technological advantages in marketing that The Secret has today, it also became an enormous success based largely on word-of-mouth. And as we'll see, intentional or not, The Secret shares some of the same marketing qualities that helped make est a worldwide phenomenon.

The Product

Though The Secret is distributed in both book and DVD form, one could say the real product being sold is the Law of Attraction itself.

While The Secret is introducing many people to this product for the very first time, the Law of Attraction has actually been bandied about for at least 100 years. The first mention of it by this name may have been back in1906 with William Walker Atkinson's book, *Thought Vibration or the Law of Attraction in the Thought World*. Still, the notion behind the Law of Attraction, that our thoughts create our lives, can be traced back at least as far as biblical times. As Solomon wrote, "As a man thinketh in his heart, so shall he be."

So, truly, there is absolutely nothing new being offered in The Secret. This makes its astonishing success even more surprising. But as we will soon see, the Law of Attraction is no ordinary product. It has a number of very appealing qualities from the consumer's perspective as well as the marketer's. We will come back to explore these in much more detail in just a bit.

The Brand

Though there are a number of well-established "brand names" in the self-help field, most of them share the names of the individuals upon whom they are based. Zig Ziglar, Anthony Robbins, and Brian Tracy are just a few examples. Given the personality driven nature of this industry, brand names that aren't tied to individuals are much more difficult to establish.

And yet, as a brand, The Secret has virtually overtaken all others in the field in little more than a year. Couple this with the fact that the product itself, the Law of Attraction, was an old, if not largely forgotten, product and we are left with quite a mystery as to its appeal. But ironically, in no small part, mystery *is* its appeal.

In wrapping the Law of Attraction up in a grand story of conspiracy, power, magic and riches, and then dubbing it *"The Secret,"* Rhonda Byrne created what may turn out to be the best-known brand the self-help field has ever seen.

"The Secret is not only a brand, but a mega-brand. Just as Xerox owned the category of instant paper duplication machines, The Secret owns a new-age concept often referred to as The Law of Attraction." Ben Mack, author of *Think Two Products Ahead*

The Marketers

Though the participants in the film are often referred to as teachers, they can also be seen as marketers. And seeing them in this way will help reveal some otherwise hidden advantages they bring to the film.

The selection of people who appear in the film was brilliant on a number of levels. While we are told that Rhonda Byrne, the film's producer, sought out people alive today who knew "the Secret," intentional or not, she also ended up with people who brought much more to the table.

First, with few exceptions, each of these teachers brought with them a cluster, if not an army, of loyal followers. As a result, as soon as the movie was finished, these followers were among the first in line to watch their idols make their big debut.

Second, with few exceptions, the individuals featured have many years of experience working the New Age market and building connections within it. And given the credibility each stood to gain if the film was a success, it should come as no surprise that so many of them hit the promotional circuit hard and heavy.

118

These individuals, who reportedly were not paid for their participation in the movie nor for promoting it, have embarked on a media blitz with appearances on major television networks, granting interviews to national media outlets such as *Newsweek* and *Time*, and even appearing on talk shows such as *Larry King Live*, *Ellen* and *Oprah*. All of this exposure is essentially free advertising for The Secret as well as valuable exposure for its teachers.

And finally, these teachers offer role models to whom viewers may look up to and aspire to be like. Almost without exception, these individuals come across as well-spoken, confident, charismatic and, most important of all, unusually successful.

One reason these individuals may appear to be so extraordinary in these areas is because, according to the Law of Attraction, they rarely speak of anything that isn't positive.

Though they may in fact fail often in their business dealings, we aren't likely to hear them speak of these failures. Though they may not always be so confident and charismatic, we aren't likely to hear this from their own lips lest they "attract" more of it into their lives.

In other words, the typical day-to-day trials and tribulations that are common in all our lives are glossed over, if these individuals mention them at all. This isn't to say that they are intentionally putting on a false front in order to deceive us. Not at all. But following the principles of the Law of Attraction and refusing to focus on negative things automatically conveys a more positive image, whether it is true or not.

The movie star Cary Grant was once asked what it was like to be larger-than-life to so many of his fans. He is reported to have responded, "We all wish we were Cary Grant. Sometimes *I* wish I was Cary Grant."

This little story illustrates the potential mistake viewers can make trying to emulate the apparent success of those we see in The Secret. The fact that we do not hear of their daily struggles does not necessarily mean they do not exist. And yet, it is so very easy to see them as larger-than-life and wonder why our own lives can't be the same.

Perhaps if we met some of these people in a more relaxed setting, they might tell us that even *they* would like to be the kind of people they seem to be onscreen.

Again, the marketing advantage provided by these participants cannot be overstated. They not only brought with them expertise; they also brought an eager and enthusiastic audience before the film had even been completed.

The Market

With millions of books and DVDs sold in less than a year, the market for The Secret is clearly enormous and appears to cut across all demographic groups. In exploring the many online community forums, we can find people from all walks of life enthusiastically practicing, supporting and spreading the word about the Law of Attraction.

This should be no surprise given the scope of the promises made in the movie – by using the Law of Attraction you can have, do and be *anything* you like. This is such a broad claim that you might think it would come across as simply nonsense to most people. But The Secret doesn't stop with promises alone. It also takes great pains to establish the "scientific validity" of its claims, thus giving it just enough clout to make believers out of millions of frustrated people. And as we'll see later, in their efforts to sustain their new beliefs and the optimism that comes with them, many of these new believers unwittingly become evangelists for the film and its stars, bringing even more people into the fold.

However, no matter how many millions of people eventually buy into the ideas presented in The Secret, there are a growing number of people who are skeptical of them. And yet, even those skeptical of the Law of Attraction and The Secret are playing a key role in helping market and build support for the film.

"Our goal is not to convert the skeptics." John Assaraf, *Larry King Live*, March 8, 2007

One reason those involved in The Secret may not be out to convert the skeptics is that doing so would prove to be exceedingly difficult. Given the lack of scientific evidence or even common sense supporting their claims, they aren't likely to be very successful.

However, there are other ways for them to handle the skeptics. These ways not only help defuse their criticism of the film, but also help build further support amongst its loyal followers.

First, the people behind this film appear to suggest that the skepticism is not only unfounded, but that it is, in fact, simply more proof that the ideas presented in The Secret are revolutionary.

When Larry King asked James Ray what he thought of the critics of the film, Ray responded:

"Well, you know, it's interesting, Larry, because any time a new idea comes to the fore, it goes through three phases. It's first ridiculed. Then it's violently opposed. And then it's finally accepted as self-evident, normally after the opposition dies.

And so what we're really doing here is bringing forth a new way of thinking and behaving that some people haven't considered before. So I'm really not surprised at all." (*Larry King Live*, March 8, 2007)

This statement appears to place the Law of Attraction in the realm of other truly revolutionary ideas such as those of Galileo, Copernicus and others. After all, since their ideas were also often attacked before being accepted as "self-evident," doesn't it make sense that the Law of Attraction would as well?

And so not only does Ray appear to defuse the criticism, but appears to have *bolstered* the credibility of his claims. However, upon closer investigation, it is easy to see that his argument, which is actually a paraphrase of one offered by the philosopher Arthur Schopenhauer – "All truth passes through three stages. First, it is ridiculed. Second, it is violently opposed. Third, it is accepted as being self-evident" – says *nothing* about the credibility of ideas being criticized. Though new ideas *may* go through these stages before they are accepted as true, it does not follow that all new ideas that are ridiculed and criticized are ultimately accepted as self-evident.

Another way they use criticism to bolster support for the film is to suggest that the critics simply don't understand the Law of Attraction. They suggest that critics haven't studied it enough, used it enough or given it a fair chance before dismissing it. As a result, the criticism is not only unfounded, it is also a sign the critics are somehow closed-minded and/or unenlightened. This suggests, by default, that the supporters of the film are just the opposite.

In a very real way, it doesn't matter whether a given person is in favor of, against or even indifferent to the film. Given the structure of the message and the marketplace, that person can be used to benefit the film, whether as a supporter, a critic or just a potential customer.

At this point, we have an established product, a hot brand, skilled marketers with built-in loyal followings and a marketplace in which nearly everyone plays an important role in the success of the film. But as we said before, the product itself – the Law of Attraction – has some additional characteristics that may also be playing a role in the success of The Secret.

The Product - Revisited

From a marketer's perspective, think about some of the characteristics a perfect product might have.

A perfect product would be easy and inexpensive to obtain but could be sold for a very high price. It would be simple to prepare for market, flexible enough to appeal to a large number of consumers, and it would encourage repeat business. It would also be a product that carried little risk to the marketer and provided great perceived value to the consumer. And finally, the perfect product would be one that satisfied customers would love to talk about.

Let's see how the Law of Attraction might compare.

The Law of Attraction is an idea that costs nothing to obtain and yet can be packaged in a way that makes it seem extremely valuable. It can then be offered in various forms and products such as books, DVDs and seminars that can be sold at premium prices.

Given its claims of being able to provide anything we could possibly want, it quite literally has universal appeal. Not only can we have, do, or be anything we want, we are told that by using the Law of Attraction, "We are the creators of our universe." In short, we will be like gods. Soon, however, students will discover that it takes time and practice to learn how to "master" the Law of Attraction so additional purchases in the form of advanced programs, coaching and seminars "may" be necessary.

Unlike most products, the consumer assumes responsibility for the effectiveness and results he or she obtains by using the Law of Attraction. This is due to the philosophy itself – the idea that each of us is responsible for everything we have "attracted" into our lives. If it turns out the Law of Attraction does not work for us, it isn't the fault of the product or its peddler; it is our fault. Maybe we didn't try hard enough, didn't think clearly enough or didn't want to achieve our goal badly enough. Whatever the reason, we can rest assured the Law of Attraction isn't to blame as we have been told it works every time, all the time, no exceptions. So whatever the reason, we are unlikely to ask for a refund and, instead, may opt for additional training.

And finally, the Law of Attraction – especially when framed as *"The Secret"* – lends itself to tremendous word-of-mouth for two reasons. One is obvious. The other is not. The first is simply the fact that many people feel compelled to share secrets. As Benjamin Franklin once said, "Three can keep a secret if two of them are dead." The second reason is less obvious, but may even be more important.

Supporters of The Secret often describe the way they felt after viewing the film in glowing terms. They may say they were overjoyed, felt empowered or that their lives had just been transformed. This euphoria may be one reason there are reports of individuals claiming to have watched the film dozens and sometimes hundreds of times. This state bears a striking resemblance to what the psychologist Abraham Maslow referred to as a peak experience:

"The person in peak-experiences feels himself, more than other times, to be the responsible, active, creating center of his activities

124

and of his perceptions. He feels more like a prime-mover, more self-determined (rather than caused, determined, helpless, dependent, passive, weak, bossed). He feels himself to be his own boss, fully responsible, fully volitional, with more 'free-will' than at other times, master of his fate, an agent." (Abraham Maslow, *Toward a Psychology of Being*)

According to the writer Colin Wilson, Maslow discovered that by simply talking about one's past peak experiences, one actually *had* more peak experiences. In an interview with The Intuition Network, Wilson had this to say about Maslow's students:

"...as soon as they began talking about their peak experiences to another and discussing them all the time, they began having peak experiences all the time."

Given this, it should be no mystery why many supporters of the film not only watch it repeatedly, but seem to talk of it incessantly; it may be one of the best ways to keep the euphoria they feel alive. Of course, from the film's perspective, it is some of the most powerful and effective word-of-mouth advertising possible.

However, even with all of these things going for it, given the many claims being made on its behalf, the Law of Attraction is prone to generate skepticism. So those marketing it must take great care to make the claims believable.

One way they do this is by filling the movie with a wide range of "experts" from metaphysicians, philosophers, entrepreneurs, feng shui consultants, visionaries and more. There is, quite literally, an expert that can satisfy most any type of viewer.

Another way is by suggesting that the Law of Attraction is somehow responsible for the successes of some of our greatest historical figures. Plato, Emerson, Shakespeare, Edison, Churchill, etc. Though The Secret never says exactly how these figures used the law, by simply suggesting they did appears to bolster the claims made on its behalf.

But the most powerful way they establish credibility for their claims is by presenting them as being based on, and even proven by, science. Some of these claims are made explicitly by calling it a universal law and stating it is as reliable as the law of gravity, for example. Other claims are made indirectly throughout the film by frequently showing images of scientific equipment and symbols such as high-tech labs, models of the atom, models of the human brain, biofeedback equipment, and even stethoscopes as their team of experts discuss the merits of the law.

In his book, *Conjuring Science: Scientific Symbols and Cultural Meanings in American Life*, Christopher Toumey warns us,

"The usual symbols of science...are vulnerable to being expropriated by causes and ideologies that have little or nothing to do with science. The result is that various movements, parties, and interest groups can bestow the plenary authority of science on their own private meanings. With a little creativity in the art of conjuring, any group can make its views seem scientific."

Though there is little doubt that the ideas taught in The Secret have been influenced by, and even inspired by, the field of quantum physics, this doesn't necessarily mean they have anything to do with quantum physics. Still, it appears for many viewers, this is exactly the message that is being conveyed.

Similarities Between *The Secret* and the est Training

Though The Secret may turn out to be the most popular and successful self-help movement of all time, it certainly isn't the first self-help super movement.

126

In the early 1970s, a phenomenon called "the est Training," which was pioneered by Werner Erhard who split off from the Church of Scientology, exploded onto the scene. Without the benefit of today's technology and without paid advertising, within just a few short years the est Training became an international sensation. Like The Secret today, est became the darling of the media and many celebrities such as Valerie Harper, John Denver and Roy Scheider attended and supported its teachings.

Though est has long since faded from the scene (it evolved into the Landmark Forum), it has been estimated that as many as a million people attended the training. And again, like The Secret, this success was due almost entirely to word-of-mouth.

Include the Landmark Forum and you have millions!

While there are a number of significant differences between these two self-help powerhouses, they do share several characteristics that may have played a large role in their success.

The first is the element of mystery.

In the case of The Secret, not only does the name of the film itself tend to evoke widespread curiosity in the public, so does the story of conspiracy and intrigue the movie tells about the Law of Attraction. Who knew this secret? How did they use it? Why did they try to keep it from the masses? Whether or not this story has any basis in fact, there is no denying its appeal.

The est Training also came with a similar element of mystery. Its mystery was simply known as "it." People who took the training were said to have gotten "it" and as a result, their lives had been transformed. They were now in charge of their own lives and seemed to have the confidence and enthusiasm to back it up. But what was "it"? No one really knew. Or at least, no one really said. "It" was something that you had to experience. "It" was something that couldn't be put into words. And the only way you could understand "it" was to attend the est training yourself.

Though "it" eventually came to be understood by many as a state of enlightenment, the mystery played a critical role in building the buzz and excitement about the training.

Another common element is the promise of "magic."

The est Training was said to, "…transform your ability to experience living so that the problems or situations in life that you are trying to solve or are putting up with will clear up just in the process of life itself." For many people, this meant the training would teach them how to easily make all their problems go away. In other words, they believed it would give them magical abilities.

In a similar fashion, according to the official website, The Secret promises, "the secret to unlimited joy, health, money, relationships, love, youth: everything you have ever wanted." In short, The Secret promises to make us gods.

Now this is quite a "step up" from the promises made by the est Training and we might be tempted to think that it would be stretching our sense of believability a little too far. But it appears that just the opposite is the case. Not only have millions already bought into The Secret, it appears millions more are waiting in the wings.

And finally, another common characteristic of the est Training and The Secret is the mechanism by which they maintain the loyalty of their supporters.

The est Training was notorious for insisting that its graduates "share" their est experiences with others and "invite" them to free events in order to learn more about the training. As a result, many of the graduates became, in essence, unpaid recruiters.

128

Though The Secret does mention the importance of sharing its message with others, it isn't mandated as it was in est. Still, as with Maslow's students, many supporters of this film seem to find that talking about the positive experiences they've had because of the film helps them *have* more positive experiences because of the film. As a result, their sharing becomes spontaneous and ever increasing as they search for their next peak experience.

Though there are other similarities between these two movements, it is difficult to underestimate the role that mystery, magic and having the right mechanism have played in their success.

And while it may be tempting to believe that the success of The Secret is due to the power of attraction, as we've seen, the power of marketing may have played an even greater role. Some may see these ideas as ushering in a "new era for humankind," but others see them for what they are. As Heinz R. Pagels was quoted as saying earlier,

"What we find here is a kind of marketplace – a reality marketplace."

And it appears that business is booming.

Chapter Nine
How To Think and Communicate With Those
Whose Feet Are Firmly Planted...
(BB)

A little boy grew up in the country and always loved turtles. To him, they were the most special of God's little creatures. He marveled at their strong back and their ability to stay safe in the wilderness. In high school the boy took a philosophy class where they talked about metaphysics and the search for the underlying structure that supports the Universe.

Being a simple country boy, he winced at obscure explanations like monism, deism, theism and Oneness. When he wrote his term paper, he found it far simpler to explain the support of the universe in his own way. The professor was stunned to read his paper and brought the boy in for conversation. Here is a sample of their dialogue:

Prof: So, you are saying that turtles are the beginning and end of all creation?
Student: Yes, it's what I've always believed.
Prof: Therefore, you do not think planet earth is supported by gravity?
Student: No, it rests on the back of a turtle.
Prof: And what does that turtle rest on?
Student: It rests on the back of another turtle.
Prof: And what does that turtle rest on?
Student: I know what you're thinking, so I'll save you some time; its turtles all the way down.

--My rendition of an old joke

Rhonda Byrne went to a lot of trouble and expense and gathered a host of experts to spread the Secret's truth. Already, Web chatter is increasing with countless people attempting to out-argue their teaching and deny the Law of Attraction. And already magazines and talk shows and churches are lining up with more counter-arguments.

There are quantum physicists who endorse The Secret, but Newsweek writes "on a scientific level, the Law of Attraction is preposterous" and the two people identified as quantum physicists are "on the fringes of mainstream science".

Smart people "know" that the Law of Attraction brought them the BMW and the huge house. Other smart people "know" that the BMW and mansion came from hard work and world-class skill.

We all know it and at times, alas, we live the following truth—arguments are almost useless. And so we may ask, "What is the point of book reviews or books like this one when people seldom change their minds and are not very easily swayed by other people's opinions?"

One of the things we can do is simply quote the following, as one reviewer did on Amazon.com:

"For those who believe, no explanation is necessary,
for those who don't, no explanation is possible."

Not a bad quote. The trouble is—it works for both sides. The skeptics of The Secret believe in, say, the eradicable nature of evil and do not want victims blamed. For that belief they can say:

"For those who believe, no explanation is necessary,
for those who don't, no explanation is possible."

Since The Secret quoted the following people, we should remind ourselves that Plato, Jesus, Lincoln, and Churchill did a lot more than just give up on all opponents and utter a one-liner. Plato, for example, was a genius at argument; Jesus' parables are stunning in their shrewd disarming of opponents; Lincoln's and Churchill's speeches swayed nations to their side.

Of course, we all have to decide when arguments are useless—and that is often a lot sooner than we think.

Since this sad fact is true, using the dialogue about The Secret as an example, we shall offer you,

A Crash Course ....
in Communicating with People Who Have Deeply Held Beliefs

The first criteria in reason and argument is to know your stuff, and just as important, to understand the position of your opponent.

One positive reviewer of The Secret suggested that many of the negative reviewers had not even seen the DVD. In that case, we can all remember one of the Ten Commandments: "Thou shalt not bear false witness against thy neighbor".

Paul Upham, a businessman from Pawling, NY was the national debating champion in his college days. Debate is high-class argument. When asked how he won the national title, he said: "I knew the position of my opponents better than they did."

In this respect, the creators and purveyors of the DVD did a poor job in anticipating the objections of their critics, especially the glaring slap in the face to the poor and oppressed of the world. It is easy to see why they did a lousy job in anticipating objections. In all of the books and articles that I have read by followers of The

Secret, there is *no* argument. Things are simply stated as if they are obvious truths and there are few back-up explanations, if any, and no real mounting of evidence.

Consider the following statements made in "The Secret to Health" section of The Secret:

"Our body is really the product of our thoughts" (p. 125).
"Disease cannot live in a body that's in a healthy emotional state." (p. 130)
"Western society has become fixated on age, and in reality there is no such thing." (p. 131)

No evidence is given for these claims. Nor do they even anticipate the simplest objection—for example, that some of them are looking a little "long in the tooth" on the DVD. If there's no such thing as age, how come some of them are looking more than a little old? (Maybe they would argue that they learned The Secret too late.)

Perhaps the most glaring example of unsubstantiated claims is, "Food is not responsible for putting on weight. It is your *thought* that food is responsible for putting on weight that actually has food put on weight." And, "Think perfect thoughts and the result must be perfect weight." Rhonda Byrne wrote this and she thinks it is "complete balderdash" that food is responsible for weight gain (p. 58, 59).

If this were not so manifestly absurd, I could well see scientists weeping whose work for The South Beach Diet or Weight Watchers or Dr. Perricone's weight loss diet is now revealed as a thorough waste of time. No need to have studied and researched trans fat and carbs and sugars and molecular reactions complex enough to boggle even their minds—no, all we need do is "think thin thoughts".

I have a friend whose life abounds in misery through no fault of her own. Her mind is filled with depressing thoughts because her husband is critically ill and unemployed, because she was fired because of a greedy boss, and because they have no money. She gained weight because she ate too much food—food being one of her only comforts. But in the last year she lost 68 lbs. even though her feeling state was one of almost constant misery. She did not lose the weight because her mind was filled with "thin thoughts". She lost it because she has some sort of stomach blockage and has eaten only cheerios and a little Ensure for the past year. She is living proof that you can feel absolutely negative and still lose weight—because food, not just thought, is the major reality when it comes to weight gain or loss.

There are many more examples of assertion without evidence. We are told that, "Abraham, Isaac, Jacob, Joseph, Moses, and Jesus were not only prosperity teachers, but also millionaires themselves, with more affluent lifestyles than many present-day millionaires could conceive of." Again, no evidence is given other than to go read *The Millionaires of the Bible Series* by Catherine Ponder (p. 109).

It would amaze every church historian, theologian, and Biblical scholar I have ever studied to hear that Jesus was a millionaire—when his own self-proclaimed statements were that he didn't even have a bed on which to lay his head. (And I bet, whatever the wealth of Abraham, most modern day millionaires would prefer a Benz to a camel, a private jet to a horse, and a fridge to something buried in the sand).

We are also told:

"It is as easy to manifest one dollar as it is to manifest one million dollars."

"You are the most powerful transmission tower in the universe." (p. 11)

"The only reason any person does not have enough money is because they are blocking money from coming to them with their thoughts." (p. 99)

"It takes no time for the Universe to manifest what you want. Any time delay you experience is due to your delay in getting to the place of believing, knowing and feeling that you already have it." (p.63)

"Praising and blessing dissolves all negativity, so praise and bless your enemies." (p. 152).

To most people, these assertions would not seem grounded in reality. For example, though all of the leading experts in wealth building would agree that we need to develop a money consciousness, there is a lot more than thoughts in the way. There is marketplace reality (a baseball player makes more than a Walmart salesperson), sweeping economic realities (the Depression, wars, the price of a barrel of oil), and unique historical and scientific circumstances (the discovery of electricity did a number on the candle business!).

Likewise, historians estimate that it takes at least a generation for a people to get over a massive assault on their civilization (e.g. the rebuilding of Beirut will have to begin again after the recent Israeli bombing). To think that praise and blame dissolves all negativity is dangerous advice in the Middle East where "your enemy never sleeps".

What is amazing about the followers of The Secret is that they are so in love with thought, but they offer little thinking. It is almost all sweeping assertions, beliefs announced as fact, and opinions

136

stated with the utmost certainty. There is virtually no wrestling with the opposing viewpoints.

And, given their view of the human mind, we have a right to expect more from them. Rhonda Bryne states that, though she never took science and physics she could understand quantum physics because she wanted to (p. 156). We are told, "You are all wisdom. You are all intelligence." (p. 164) and, "You are a genius beyond description." (p. 171) and, "As you become aware of the power of The Secret, and begin to use it, all of your questions will be answered." (p. 171).

If that isn't enough to hope for better reasoning from them, then we can fall back on their promise that, "if you are seeking an answer or guidance on something in your life, ask the question, believe you will receive, and then open this book randomly. At the exact place where the pages fall open will be the guidance and answer you are seeking." (p. 172).

Needless to say, this assertion can never be out argued because they can always say I never really sought the answer or believed their answer once I opened the page. But since, "I am all genius" and know that I really want an answer to the question, "Why does The Secret contain little reasoning?" I am going to close my eyes, open the book and point to a spot on the page. Ready? Here comes the answer:

"When you want to attract something in your life, make sure your actions don't contradict your desires." (p. 115).

That is not bad advice at all, but I cannot really see how it answers my question. Those who know philosophy and belief systems and cults will agree with a far more obvious answer: The Secret is the most glaring example of "it's turtles all the way down" we have come across in years.

At this juncture, let's examine whether the followers of The Secret really know their stuff when it comes to the list of historical figures that presumably knew the Secret. We will look extensively at Jesus in a later chapter—but The Secret clearly states that the Law of Attraction was known and delivered by Shakespeare, Browning, Blake, Beethoven, da Vinci, Socrates, Plato, Emerson, Pythagoras, Bacon, Newton, Goethe, and Victor Hugo (p.4).

As a general reply, anyone who has been educated in the history of philosophy, literature, and music will be quite surprised to learn that these people believed the Law of Attraction. Victor Hugo's *Les Miserables*, Goethe's *The Sorrow of Young Werther*, Shakespeare's *King Lear*, and Plato's dialogues all have a far more gritty, negative explanation for the miseries of this world than that we attract negativity. There are evil children, greedy businessmen, jealous lovers, selfish governments and sociopathic kings. In Shakespeare, "life doth make cowards of us all" because life is often a fear-inducing reality, as the rebels in *Les Miserables* discovered as they confronted the armies of France.

I am not musically talented or trained (not even as a historian of music), so I find myself hard pressed how one could figure out whether Beethoven "expressed" the Law of Attraction through his music (p. 4). Beethoven actually worked very hard on his music. He spent two years writing the 8th Symphony. Research shows that he did pages and pages of rewrites in the notebooks he used for his work.

The research for The Secret appears to have been conducted in the following way. If they found a quote that at all sounded like The Secret, the writer was automatically viewed as a progenitor. If someone wrote a phrase advocating gratitude, for example, he or she is then claimed as an advocate of the Law of Attraction, despite what the rest of their writing actually says. This is called taking something "out of context". Even worse, it is not knowing the context.

Let's take a brief look at the following quotation from Ralph Waldo Emerson: "The secret is the answer to all that has been, all that is, and all that will ever be." (p. 183) It certainly sounds like the one being quoted might be an advocate of The Law of Attraction. But no such quotation can be found in The Complete Works of Ralph Waldo Emerson which can be searched on the website dedicated to his legacy—(www.rwe.org/).

The definitive biography of Emerson is *Emerson: A Mind on Fire* by Robert D. Richardson Jr. It reveals nothing which suggests that Emerson believed The Secret. His truths and feelings were honed and earned with great learning, serious struggle, intense discipline and passion almost always in step with depression and doubt. There was precious little that was easy in his journey along the lines of "like attracts like" and ask and you will get it.

Now let's look at Socrates. Here are quotations directly from his lips where he presents views that do not consider the Law of Attraction as the explanation for human well being or human destruction.

"I have incurred a great deal of bitter hostility, and this is what will bring about my destruction, if anything does—not Meletus, not Anytus, but the slander and jealousy of a very large section of the people. They have been fatal to a great many other innocent men, and I suppose will continue to be so; there is no likelihood that they will stop at me." (Socrates Defense 28a, p. 14)

"If I had tried long ago to engage in politics, I should long ago have lost my life." (Defense, 31d, p. 17)

"The mind of the good and true artist is always occupied with one thought, how justice may be implanted in the souls of the citizens and injustice banished, and how temperance may be implanted and indiscipline banished, and how goodness may be engineered and wickedness depart." (Gorgias, 504,e. p. 287)

"Unless there is a conjunction of political power and philosophical intelligence, there can be no cessation of trouble." (Republic V, 473d, p. 712-713)

"Great crimes and unmixed wickedness come from a vigorous nature corrupted by its nurture." (Republic, VI, 491 e, p. 728)

"And do you not also concur in this very point that the blame for this harsh attitude of the many towards philosophy falls on that riotous crew who have burst in where they do not belong, wrangling with one another, filled with spite, and always talking about persons, a thing least befitting philosophy." (Republic, VI, 500b, p. 735)

"There exists in every one of us, even in some reputed most respectable, a terrible, fierce and lawless brood of desires." (Republic, IX, 572b, p. 799)

"We must acknowledge disease of the mind to be a want of intelligence and of this there are two kinds—to wit, madness and ignorance." (Timaeus. 86b, p. 1206)

"Life abounds in good things, but most of those good things are infested by polluted and defiling parasites." (Laws XI, 937b, p. 1487)

The dense arguments of Socrates show not the slightest hint of any belief that is akin to the Law of Attraction. In Socrates' world our souls are corrupted by an excessive love of pleasure and power and fame, by evil men and women, by bad teaching, by lazy habits, by great art that makes evil more appealing, by dull art that makes goodness seem dull, by the power of sexual love, and a host of other pollutants.

And there is certainly not one sentence in Plato where it is entertained for a second (by even the enemies of Socrates) that the path to human well being is easy, simple and available from the Universe at the speed of light. There are no short cuts in Plato. Wisdom demands the rigorous companions of hard thinking, courage, self-discipline, honesty, a long search for experts in certain areas, and a fierce independence of soul to not be swayed by the crowd or one's wild pleasures.

Plato reminds us of **a second tool in argument—the ability to think straight**. This is a very difficult task for all kinds of reasons. Even Socrates, a master at reasoning, spoke constantly of how hard it is to find the truth, to think clearly, and to follow an argument in a fair and accurate manner. We are blinded by our passions, by our allegiance to our own viewpoints, and by what philosophers call "logical fallacies".

One logical error that often occurs in The Secret is that we are offered a false dichotomy. Here's an example:

"Do you want to believe that you can be in the wrong place at the wrong time? That you have no control over circumstances?" (p. 28)

Only a masochist would *want* to believe that you can be in the wrong place at the wrong time. But even if we don't want it—it still could be true, and appears to be from the morning newspaper. However, even if it is true that we can be in the wrong place at the wrong time, this does not mean that we have no control over circumstances.

The alternative we are given is to "want to believe and know that your life experience is in your hands and that only all good can come into your life because this is the way you think. You have a choice, and what ever you choose to think will become your life experience." (p. 28)

Again, not only is this viewpoint asserted, it also does not present a third choice—i.e., some of my life experience is in my hands and what I think does make a great deal of difference, but not all the difference.

A third tool in argument is to avoid what philosophers call "argumentum ad hominem" which means we attack the man, rather than the argument. And so on Amazon.com here is what you are told when you do not agree with the Secret:

> "Miserable ingrates…who blame others…"

> "They are skeptical or would rather live a life of misery and lack."

> "Closed minds."

> "Those who think it is garbage don't believe in miracles and have no faith."

Just the negativity of their comments is enough to make you sick.

Here is what happens if you agree with The Secret:

> "The makers of it can make money by selling dreams and hope."

> "The film and the people responsible for it are bottom-feeding trash."

> "What lazy greedy American doesn't want more stuff without actually doing something for it."

"Like religion or a support group, some people just need a little something extra."

There is no argument in the above examples. Instead, you attack the person—their motives or character or faith or lack of it. Is this a calculated distraction? Is it a sign of a weak argument, so you better attack the person? Do people get angry because their obvious truths are being questioned? Or, as we shall see in the next chapter, do we go at somebody because our precious beliefs are threatened?

One advocate for the pro Secret side quoted the Turkish proverb: "if you tell the truth, have one foot in the stirrup".

Of course the issue is: who has the truth? As you can see from Amazon, both sides need the stirrup.

A fourth tool in argument is to find common ground.

All reviewers on Amazon.com seemed pretty much on the side of gratitude, positive thinking, intentional living, and human compassion. Likewise, here is perhaps the best thought from Rhonda Bryne in The Secret: "With all that I have read and with all that I have experienced in my own life using The Secret, the power of gratitude stands above everything else. If you only do one thing with the knowledge of the Secret, use gratitude until it becomes your way of life." (p. 76. 77)

Whether you are for or against The Secret, we all need practice in gratitude and positive thinking. In fact, one of the difficult things in any type of research is to unravel what exactly helps someone in their particular belief, group, or way of life. Does The Secret work for people because it influences them to be more grateful, to be more open to serendipity, and to believe they are in a friendlier universe? All of this would have a positive effect on people even if there were no actual Law of Attraction operating in the universe.

A fifth tool in argument is to see where you opponents are coming from.

The Secret did a lousy job in fending off the obvious attack that their theory is perhaps the best blaming mechanism in history. But we can see that they were trying to share their message in a movie meant for mass appeal and in a popular book meant for every one. They did not write a philosophy book. Of course, any well-trained philosophers would have to hide theirs head in shame if they didn't logically anticipate and answer all objections. And a popular book is no excuse for sloppy logic, historical error (see their use of Socrates), and misleading implications.

The most potent tool in argument is to understand the emotional world behind your opponent. This is what marketing experts call the "sweet spot" of why someone buys into something or actually buys something. Emotions are what run human beings and we are all driven by deep, unconscious desires that are fairly universal.

For example, notice how The Secret feeds into our desire to feel special, potent, loved and effective. Or observe how the angry opponents of The Secret are driven by compassion for the ill treated of the world.

This is far from just logic.

And so when you argue, you had better know your own hot spot as well as that of your opponent.

Because two hot spots tend to create a fire.

These "hot spots" may stem from more than just a failure in logic. What if we are not smart and can't follow an argument? What if we begin to feel that we don't know our stuff as Paul Upham takes us on? What if we are distracted by the other 5,000 things our brains process every second? What if we make our living defending our truth and the mortgage is on the line?

What about intuition?

How can you argue against someone's intuition? What if Rhonda Byrne is better looking and appeals to people differently from some man who might debate her on *Larry King Live*? What if The Secret DVD is better-produced and more visually grabbing than, say, a potential competitor in the DVD world?

The world is not a level playing field for argument and discussion and debate.

We need even more help in how to think.

Chapter 10
Teaching Others How To Think
(DL)

Look this up.

As of this writing the book *Blink* (a good book) is number 197 on Amazon and the book *Think!* (a phenomenal book about thinking) is number 100,634.

Thinking, reasoning, and challenging are not valued nearly as highly as the idea that we can make the correct decisions in the blink of an eye.

Our society has come to value speed, convenience, comfort and feel-good ideologies more than hard work, critical thinking and proper action.

Which is the very reason this book will predictably under perform The Secret.

And that alone should frighten you more than all of the pseudo science and metaphysical laws of the universe combined.

For me at the end of the day it isn't that we need to fix the problems that the Law of Attraction represents, it is that we need to fix the thinking that allows these kinds of ideas to be easily accepted and proliferate.

Political correctness is an idea that started much like the Law of Attraction. It seemed like such a good idea, equality, fair play, feeling good with each other, but it turned out to be something quite different. Political Correctness is about control and litigation.

If people simply believed that they could create things with their thoughts, it really wouldn't be a problem. By necessity they'll figure out quickly enough that they can't and move on to something else. It is the deeper problem, the problem of wanting simple, fast, feel-good answers for real problems. It is the kind of thinking that has allowed many of our jobs to head overseas and our health care system to morph into what it has become today.

It is the same kind of thinking that allows people to believe that things are predestined and everything happens for a reason.

But this isn't a political commentary; it is a commentary on thinking and the Law of Attraction.

I'd really have no problem with the idea of the Law of Attraction if it were termed the "mindset of attraction" or "attraction principles". If it were presented in that way, it would simply be a way of thinking about a group of ideas that may have potential to be true or not true. It is a little like having a ritual of tying your left shoe first before you compete or whatever ritual you might use to help insure luck.

Instead, the Law of Attraction is presented as a law, a physical law like gravity, one that produces the same results exactly under the same set of conditions every time.

As a marketer, persuader and a propagandist, I understand the value of emotional language and the Law of Attraction is pure emotional language designed to make an otherwise unbelievable idea palatable. The more precise your language the more precise your message, but, sometimes by being less precise you get a much more emotional reaction. Half- baked messages are often much easier to accept than the truth and they are nearly always sexier sounding.

Don't believe me? Check out snopes.com, the single best resource on the Internet for finding out the truth about urban legends of all sorts. There are literally thousands of references to all kinds of stories, the majority of which turn out not to be true.

If you asked the people who promote the Law of Attraction if they believed that the image of the Virgin Mary burned into a grilled cheese sandwich was a real manifestation by the Virgin or proof of God's existence, they'd likely all tell you no, that it is an anomaly, a coincidence that is uncanny.

But here is what is interesting, there is an explanation: the psychological phenomenon called Pareidolia. Pareidolia is a psychological phenomenon involving a vague and random stimulus (usually an image) being mistakenly perceived as recognizable. Humans are able to find seemingly endless connections in random patterns, many that show up as faces, others that show up as messages when you listen to recordings in reverse.

But they are not real.

In fact, the most recent research around Pareidolia comes from Doris Tsao, a neurobiologist, who won the Eppendorfer/Science International prize in neurobiology for her research on face recognition in monkeys. It turns out that the same areas of the brain respond when shown faces or even cartoon faces in the monkey's brains, even when there is only the slightest facial resemblance. They (and we) are genetically wired to recognize faces.

But a much easier explanation for the masses is that the burn mark in the grilled cheese is the Virgin Mary. It works out even better if you can get a few people to come over and worship the sandwich and talk about the mystical feelings they have while they are there. They'll talk about how they felt a presence of God.

But the fact that there is a scientific explanation doesn't matter. Casinos don't buy scientific sandwiches for $28,000 but a sandwich with the face of the Virgin burned in, well, that is a completely different story . . . it has a draw, a story, people want to see it and it will get covered by the media. It has profit potential.

A lot like saying that thoughts are things and that if you think of a feather you'll attract a feather.

How Ideas Like The Law of Attraction Are Spread

Edward Bernays is credited with being the father of Public Relations. He was also Sigmund Freud's nephew and the author of a book called Propaganda.

Bernays believed that public opinion must be manipulated because manipulation was a necessary part of democracy. He felt society was irrational and dangerous. He set out and accomplished many significant changes socially; he orchestrated the pivotal event that allowed women to smoke in public.

In addition to focusing on the subconscious and the psychological testing and research of his uncle, Bernays used third party authorities to champion his clients and their ideas. He felt that, "If you can influence the leaders, either with or without their conscious cooperation, you automatically influence the group which they sway."

This is one of the single most important things that the followers of the Law of Attraction have done and with great success. They targeted very visible marketers with large followings and got them to champion the cause.

150

In Bernays' case, when he wanted to promote bacon, he surveyed a large group of doctors about the importance of a hearty breakfast and then released the study and tied it together with bacon and eggs and an example of a healthy breakfast. The Attractionists did something very similar, they found a couple of fringe scientists who are not really studying the Law of Attraction as it relates to science at all and tied them to it. Then they spoke with the teachers of the Law of Attraction and tied it to something they'd all be able to identify with, Napoleon Hill's *Think and Grow Rich*. It would be an easy sell to their audiences who were already familiar with that concept, sprinkle it with a little pseudo science, and it would be a very easy, happy pill to swallow.

Edward Bernays said: "If we understand the mechanism and motives of the group mind, is it not possible to control and regiment the masses according to our will without their knowing about it? The recent practice of propaganda has proved that it is possible, at least up to a certain point and within certain limits." (*Propaganda*, 2005 ed., p. 71.)

If you want to spread ideas that lack a valid basis you cannot be precise in your communication, you must speak in much larger ambiguous terms and the Attractionists have that down to a science.

Here is how you sell an idea of questionable value:

1. Identify the emotional lever that will fulfill a significant desire that people have; the big three being Money, Sex and Health. Find something that will help one of those and you'll be rich, find something that does all three and you'll rule the world.
2. Present the idea, support it with what appears to be factual evidence, ask them to search their own experience to find examples of what you are purporting as the truth.

3. Be ambiguous and always move them back to emotion. There is a saying that some pitchmen use when referring to audiences that they sell to, "A crier is a buyer." If you can manipulate the emotion to a point that they feel emotionally overwhelmed by their perceived loss or lack, their pain will lean them to your cure.

4. Build your crowd fast, the bigger the crowd and the faster it grows the less people will think about it. Hire crowds or shills where necessary to support your belief. Create your own studies or surveys that support your ideas.

5. Control thinking. Tell people what they must believe or do in order for your outcome to occur. Give yourself an out when possible. Good outs are those that you can attribute back to the person who isn't achieving the result you promise. In the case of the Law of Attraction, I love the out that says, "you may have a belief that you are not even aware of that is keeping you from attracting the things that you want, you may not feel worthy or deserving."

6. Provide social proof as soon as possible. Line up the testimonials. Highly charged, emotional testimonials from true believers are best.

7. Encourage the early adopters to evangelize, get them to spread the good word to everyone they know. Encourage them to form groups and networks to support each other in their new belief.

8. Inoculate them against criticism, preemptively tell them where the "unenlightened" will challenge them and provide them with responses that are carefully crafted to rebut the challengers. Tell them to disregard thinking or science or proof. Point to all the ideas that were believed to be untrue years ago (for example the belief that the world was flat) but have been disproved.

9. Make them pioneers and martyrs, the venerated heroes who suffer the slings and arrows of a benighted public afraid of change.

10. As the idea takes hold, disappear, become less available and only show up to reignite the movement or to direct it.

Follow these steps and you'll be able to create your own law and sell it to anyone you know.

One of my core problems with the whole idea of the Law of Attraction is the lack of focus on action and the willingness to promote an idea that doesn't stand up to scientific scrutiny or even simple critical thinking. Let's look at critical thinking and scientific skepticism and ask some very simple questions.

First, a couple of definitions:

Critical Thinking is a term used to refer to those kinds of mental activity that are clear, precise, and purposeful. It is typically associated with solving complex real world problems, generating multiple (or creative) solutions to a problem, drawing inferences, synthesizing and integrating information, distinguishing between fact and opinion, or estimating potential outcomes.

Scientific Skepticism is a scientific, or practical, epistemological position (or paradigm) in which one questions the veracity of claims unless they can be scientifically verified.

And finally, let's talk about beliefs because we can't talk about the Law of Attraction without discussing belief.

Belief is defined as any cognitive content held to be true.

So here are the easy questions:

1. Can the claims of the Law of Attraction be scientifically verified? To date the answer is no and in my research, I could not find anyone who was doing specific research to

153

conclusively prove the veracity of the claims related to the Law of Attraction being a real thing.

2. Is there a clear distinction between fact and opinion in the Law of Attraction? The answer is yes, but if you ask a practitioner of the law, they readily report things that sound factual but in fact are opinions, many of which originate with an entity claimed to be channeled by Esther Hicks called Abraham.

3. Is there cognitive content held to be true? The answer here is clearly yes but the content is, at least currently, inaccurate because there is no empirical evidence to back it up.

4. Does someone stand to profit greatly from the proliferation of these pseudo facts? The answer again is clearly yes and they already have.

What should be of great concern to everyone is the willingness to accept ideas without critical thinking. Blindly accepting ideas because they sound good or because you want them to be true is the basis for many of the problems that face our society today.

Let's look more closely at why the idea of the Law of Attraction sounds so good and is so easy to swallow.

People, particularly Americans are looking for quick fixes, easy solutions to life-long problems. They want to be able to feel like they are taking some proactive role in the rapidly changing world around them. They want to make sense of it all.

Along comes an idea, carefully packaged, beautifully produced and presented as if it were truth known to some of the greatest minds and greatest leaders in the world and that they somehow kept it from the masses in Illuminati-like secrecy. Amazingly though, the secret is discovered and revealed to the world by a divorced television producer in Australia.

But not to make it sound too implausible, I mean secrets get out all the time these days, turns out the secret has actually been around for hundreds of years, they just blew the dust off and repackaged it.

It turns out, that part is the only truth in The Secret.

The Secret has been around for hundreds of years. The Secret has been around since someone first figured out they could create a highly emotional response in another person and that response would cause the person on the experiencing end to shell out money or favors.

Conmen know it and prey on victims, hustlers know it and prey on the desire for a fast dollar, snake oil salesmen prey on the desire for a quick fix to physical problems. And often it doesn't matter how much the belief can be disproved, they keep going back for more because they got hooked.

Drug dealers know this and that is why they are happy to give you the first experience for free, you just pay for the rest with the rest of your life.

I'm often asked why any of this matters, why not just let this fad pass like all the rest of the many unreasonable ideas in the self help movement?

The answer is quite simple: because this one takes such a huge shot at charity, compassion, hard work and action.

Society has been built on hard work; fortunes have been made by hard work, cities built and diseases ended by hard work.

Not by wishful thinking.

The problems of the day will be solved the same way, by critical thinking and hard work.

155

Someone has to do the thinking, the acting, the building, but not someone alone; all of us as a whole have to think, focus, commit and act.

What is the answer?

I'm so glad you asked.

The answer is to slow down, take a little time and critically evaluate the information you receive. Ask penetrating questions about the validity of the claims and the promises. This works not just for ideas like the Law of Attraction but everyplace you find yourself struggling to decide what is true or not true, real or not real.

In fact, here is a list of questions that you can use to begin to better challenge ideas and beliefs to get people to clearly define what it is that they are proposing.

- How do you know?
- How do you quantify that?
- What is the proof that exists proving that?
- Are you sure that is right?
- Are you sure that is true?
- What would happen if? For example, what would happen if you used the Law of Attraction to attract a car wreck for your worst enemy?
- Can you prove that?
- How do you measure that?
- How does one prove or quantify that?
- Why is that important?
- Can you be more specific?
- What do you or does that mean?
- How specifically do you do that?

- Are you sure?
- Give me an example where that is true. Now another and now one more.
- Was there ever a time that X was true or not true? Why did it change?
- What other questions should I have asked you, but didn't?

When you ask penetrating questions, it is important to listen carefully to the answer. You have to listen for clear concise responses that provide evidence. You must also be aware of emotion, frustration, backpedaling, convolution, and other attempts to not provide a clear answer.

Earlier I spoke about a debate I had with a person who represented themselves as a teacher of the truth around the Law of Attraction. I used this exact process of questioning to get him to admit that he was selling the Law of Attraction because it is what people wanted to buy and that it was important to sell them what they wanted, not what they need. In other words, it was ok to misrepresent science and the truth if that is what people wanted.

Here is how I might question someone about the validity of the Law of Attraction.

Attractionist: Thoughts become things, I manifest physically what I think about.
Me: Are you sure?
Attractionist: Yes, just the other day I needed extra money and I started thinking, visualizing with great emotion and intent, checks coming in the mail. And lo and behold, on Thursday there was a check in the mail.
Me: Who specifically sent you the check?
Attractionist: It came from a person who owed me money but who hadn't paid me back as promised.
Me: So did you really attract it or did the person pay you back?

Attractionist: The person paid me back but he did it after I started thinking about it.

Me: How are you sure he didn't intend to pay you back before you started to think about it?

Attractionist: It doesn't matter; I thought it and the money came.

Me: It did come after you thought about it. Did you ever think about wanting that person to pay you before and it didn't come?

Attractionist: Well yes, but I was angry that he wasn't paying me and had a "lack mentality," that is the reason that it didn't come. But now that I understand the Law of Attraction, I just know money will come when I need it.

Me: Could we test this?

Attractionist: Sure!

Me: Great, please choose an amount of money that you'd like to attract within a specific period of time. It must be above and beyond all the normal income that you'll have coming in during that time period from investments, your paycheck etc. and we won't count any money owed to you that hasn't been paid unless you are expecting the payment as part of your normal income.

Attractionist: I'm not sure that is how the Law of Attraction works and it won't prove that the Law of Attraction doesn't work if I don't attract the money.

Me: It will prove that the Law of Attraction didn't work this time and, if it doesn't work this time, then you have to question the premise of the belief which is that it works every time no matter what.

Attractionist: I don't think the test makes sense, I just know that it is true and surrounding myself with negativity like that will just attract more negativity to me. I know it works and that is what is important to me.

Me: Can you give me other specific examples where the Law of Attraction has worked, examples that have been published in peer reviewed scientific journals?

Attrationist: No but I'm sure they exist.

The conversation can go on for a very long time but eventually the Attractionist must fall back on the idea that they simply have faith that it is real and they accept it at that.

And it would seem like this is a futile argument, but in reality what you've done is cause doubt and drive a wedge in their thinking. You've made them aware of times when the Law of Attraction isn't working and the more conscious they become of the variances from their expectations, the more likely they are to take a harder look at what they believe and ask tougher questions on their own.

The real value in challenging ideas like this is not to convince the person with the idea that he is wrong, it is to make him think.

One of the most important things that you can do for yourself, your family, your community and our society is to learn more about critical thinking and practice it always. Go back to the definition of critical thinking, it incorporates challenging, reasoning, thinking creatively and expansively, but it leads you back to narrowing your thoughts down to something usable and provable.

Use these guides to critical thinking as you navigate the ideas you are presented with on a daily basis.

- Strive to distinguish fact from opinion
- Assess the reliability of the source
- Validate the accuracy of a statement
- Separate relevant from irrelevant information
- Listen for and detect bias
- Identify unstated assumptions
- Recognize logical inconsistencies

Now, think.

- Define the problem
- Evaluate the information related to the problem
- Draw your conclusions and develop possible solutions
- Devise and Implement a plan of action
- Review your results, reflect, and when necessary begin again

Interestingly, when you follow this process, thoughts do become things . . . because you actually take the necessary actions to turn the thought into something tangible and make the necessary corrections to insure success.

Let me leave you with this little exercise. Practice critical thinking for a week. Simply challenge the things around you that pique your interest, ideas that don't seem quite right, and see what you discover.

I think you'll be pleasantly and likely profitably surprised by the results.

The problem with feel-good quick fixes is that they don't hold for very long. To choose not to think critically is to choose to fail. For a society to willingly suspend its disbelief and gladly put on blinders is unforgivable. It is a recipe for disaster.
Expect more of yourselves and each other.

Chapter Eleven
How to Change—or, the Real Reason Behind The Secret's Appeal
(BB)

There are at least 60 books and dozens of websites that endorse the Law of Attraction mindset. *Newsweek* magazine lists 9 major "progenitors of positivity" to the New Thought movement, ranging from Phineas Quimby in the 19th century to Norman Vincent Peale and Tony Robbins in the 20th century. Imagine if you read all this and nothing else?

Chances are you would be "under the spell" of such a massive infusion of energy and thought, even if you disagreed with it.

And there are at least 60 books and dozens of websites that attack the Law of Attraction and the New Thought movement. Imagine if you read all *this* and nothing else?

Chances are you would be "under the spell" of such a massive infusion of energy and thought, even if you disagreed with it.

What if you read everything from both sides? What if the authors of this book read everything from both sides?

This illustrates a vital point at the heart of influence and persuasion and change. To know something and to properly evaluate it, we really need to give our attention to it. More importantly, to be *changed* by something we really need to give our attention to it. We need to be students and perhaps devotees of the subject at hand. And even if we do not want to be a devotee, we are subliminally influenced by how our attention is taken—for example, by the media!

This is the first complex reality we alluded to in the previous chapter. Who has time for such diligence and devotion in pursuing just one subject matter?

Furthermore, who has the time to investigate and be changed by all the "truths" and belief systems that are offered to us? There are 7 major world religions, 3 major branches of Christianity (Roman Catholic, Protestant, and Orthodox), 3 major branches of Judaism (orthodox, conservative and reform), at least a dozen major psychotherapy traditions (Freud, cognitive therapy, object relations, systemic therapy, etc. etc) and all kinds of other alternative paths of healing.

Thankfully, there is still only 1 partridge in a pear tree and you may know whether to brush your teeth from side to side rather than up and down.

But have you heard about the following movements or solutions that also offer you the key to enlightenment: Amway, NLP, EMDR, hypnosis, marriage retreats, colonics, bluegreen algae, breathwork, Rolfing, Adidam, Urantia, Priory of Sion, Raelians, Sai Baba, Falun Gong, Osho (Rajneesh), Ahmadiyya, and The Way International.

Even within a confined world there are divisions and differences. Certain Christians believe the Bible is infallible, others believe the Pope is infallible, while still other Christians think that the Bible contains the Word of God. There are about 2,000 different groups of Baptists in the world alone.

For each of us, there is a mountain of material that offers to change us and we are already overwhelmed and confused by the marketplace of choices.

And if we give our time to investigating the Secret and allowing ourselves to be influenced by its charm, we are then automatically saying no to other seductresses. We do not have the time to investigate all possibilities. We cannot pay attention to everything.

But all of this is nothing compared to the next complex reality.

All of us are already in a "sort of" cult. Now we mean this here in a looser sense than will be examined in the next chapter. But in this loose sense, the history of each of us is the history of all the cults in which we have belonged. A cult is, supposedly, a small group of believers who think some strange things. How could you be part of a cult?

This is what happened to all of us as we grew up. Our attention was taken by the "truths" we were taught by our parents, siblings, society, teachers, clergy, friends, relatives and the extraordinary and ordinary events of our lives. We gave all our time to these lessons and we did not even know it was happening! We are all victims of the most persuasive process in the world—our childhoods.

Most people do not question their upbringing until adolescence. But even our adolescence is a brainwashing phenomenon— the particulars depending on where you are from and whether you hang around people from the Jesus Camp, your fellow cocaine addicts, or the local Mensa group.

And it does not end there. Here is one probable history: totally consumed and devoted to sex (male view: age 13 to 90), committed to one belief system up to 13; at least a minor absorption in alcohol and drugs, major devotion to the creation of your career (acrobat in Cirque de Soleil), divorce (age 36-38, feels like you are having a car accident every day), start to realize that money matters (35-50), begin to know you have joints and that our bodies really matter (age 40-90); panic at the coming horizon and focus exclusively on your new novel as the legacy of legacies (age 55-70)—no time for the Secret now. Hopefully the Secret works, because there is no time to lose (age 70 to 90).

Who can get around the internal programming called our life?

We are all wedded to our past and we each have our cherished beliefs, attitudes, practices, habits and opinions.

Changing our lives is like being on a boat in the middle of the ocean and perhaps (perhaps!) realizing that we need a new boat. But we can't go back to shore. And so we have to build a new boat while steering the old boat. We can never entirely get rid of the old boat—because it contains our body, our language, the treasures from our past, our memories—and yet we need a new boat. How do we know what is the best new boat?

What do we do? Marketing experts and psychologists tell us that it comes to one simple question: where is your pain? If you are very content with your life, you are probably not reading this book or viewing The Secret. If you need to lose weight, you are probably now reading a book on carbs. If you have a miserable sex life, you might be reading about Tantric sex. If you have a disease, you are searching everywhere.

In our lives, our emergency mode can get us searching in a specific area for a cure, an answer, some relief, some hope, some insight, and a solution to our pain. Given all the problems in life and all the growth options available, we need to work as fast as possible.

But do we?

We ignore, deny, pretend, procrastinate, focus on other people's problems, and have about 50 ways to not face ourselves in the mirror or truly examine the proposed solutions to our problem. We resist new truth and cling to life as we know it.

People even avoid the warning signs of a heart attack as they dismiss the winded breathing and the pain in the left arm.

In the psychiatric world these are called "defense mechanisms". There are about twenty-five major defense mechanisms and twenty-nine minor defense mechanisms according to H.P. Laughlin in his classic work, *The Ego and Its Defenses.* You can read that three hundred and thirty two page book after your Law of Attraction research or you can shorten your workload by listening to Shakespeare: "We would rather bear those ills we have, than fly to those we know not of, thus life doth make cowards of us all."

You are probably beginning to think that we need to find an expert! But this is not a guarantee that we will head in the right direction either! Which expert? Experts have their own childhoods, their own adolescence, their own unique history, and their own defense mechanisms.

No wonder we all erase a lot of options very quickly. There is no time to do anything else but that—for almost everything in the world.

However, The Secret comes along and **it takes no time to learn. It is a simple, supposedly fast acting alternative for those overwhelmed in the marketplace of choices. This is one of the secret explanations of its appeal. It is presented as an easy shortcut to success and a quick detour around the misery of life.**

But the authors of The Secret also have their own childhood, adolescence, unique history and defense mechanisms.

If this isn't enough, what if we examine what part religion plays in this picture?

Chapter Twelve
Is the Secret A Cult?
(DL)

One of the things that I'm often asked is whether or not the Law of Attraction or The Secret is a cult.

And the answer is yes . . . but with some qualification. Most religions could be defined as a cult but more specifically Practitioners of The Secret and The Law of Attraction have formed an ideological (to date) cult following with a leaning toward a religious cult.

There are three definitions of a cult that I'll use as the basis for discussing the Law of Attraction cult.

1. An instance of great veneration of a person, ideal, or thing, esp. as manifested by a body of admirers – dictionary.com – Unabridged edition
2. Obsessive, especially faddish, devotion to or veneration for a person, principle, or thing – American Heritage Dictionary
3. The object of such devotion – American Heritage Dictionary

I'm going to focus to a lesser extent on definition one and more on definition two and three.

First of all, do I think that The Secret and The Law of Attraction represent a destructive cult? The answer is yes and no.

To the extent that authorities presenting the Law of Attraction, specifically those who are featured in the seminal work around the Law of Attraction today, The Secret, teach that subconsciously people including children are attracting things like rape, murder, genocide, and disease to themselves, it becomes destructive. To the further extent that they promote an absolute idea of, "Ask, Believe, Receive" as a means of getting anything you want, it is also emotionally harmful to those people for whom the formula doesn't work.

There is a significant difference between optimism (which is a tendency to expect the best possible outcome in a situation) and the kind of thinking that says your thoughts become things and if you don't think well enough you won't be rewarded. Even worse, if you think bad things, they'll come true.

In many cults there is an exalted leader that everyone worships. And to counter the idea that the Law of Attraction is a cult the practitioners regularly point out that there is no centralized leadership, that there was no revealed truth.

But nothing could be further from the truth.

The Law of Attraction principles as defined today are widely attributed to Esther Hicks, the human that channels the spirit being Abraham who dispenses esoteric wisdom through his earthly mouthpiece. And while there has been a falling out between the producers of The Secret and her, they still acknowledge her ideas as being pivotal in Law of Attraction thinking.

Additionally, The Secret and the venerated teachers in the movie have been placed on a pedestal. Their beliefs and ideology become the beliefs of the members who follow them. When those leaders speak from the stage or from television they are identified as the true holders and practitioners of the Law of Attraction and the followers listen and take action. The overt articulation is that the best of the best were chosen and the followers follow their leaders. . . .Unquestioningly.

In addition, to learn The Secret, you must buy The Secret. Even churches, where there is much to criticize, don't charge you to attend and learn their version of the truth. So more and more criteria stack up that add up to a cult following . . . and I haven't even begun to discuss the advanced training that costs up to $1995.00 so far.

Now, don't get me wrong, I'm an unabashed marketer. I have no problem with people creating a product and selling it for whatever people will pay for it. I do it every day. But, when you begin to say that you are selling revealed truth and secrets, it puts you in another category.

All of The Secret teachers are positioning themselves both subtly and overtly to be seen as having all the truth (which is for sale or will come in The Secret 2). They are all actively trying to create a following of worshipers.

Again, I don't have a problem with developing an ethical cult following, I teach people how to do it.

But when they develop a following around mystical, unproven or untested, and non-scientific ideas that they pass off as the truth, then there is a problem.

Let's look at some of the elements of a destructive cult and see if you notice any similarities between these ideas and The Secret.

- Create a front, put all the helpful information right up front, hide the insidiousness – The Secret uses the Law of Attraction, a simple, seductive idea to suck people in. Once they buy into the idea that they can create all the material wealth they need, they don't notice or more easily accept the more obviously problematic ideas.

- Deceive and distort the truth, don't tell the truth about yourself – In the movie itself some of the teachers are given official sounding titles to cover for their lack of scientific credibility. Give the teachers big names like Philosopher or Visionary.

- Create a façade – In this case the façade is that the Law of Attraction is based on physics.

- Promise to fulfill their dreams and help them find a version of salvation – The Law of Attraction itself fills this idea: your thoughts become physical things, you can think anything you want into existence, you are all powerful.

- Give to receive their support – Blogs, "free" courses, teleseminars all were used leading into the launch of The Secret to begin spreading the idea of the Law of Attraction.

- Distort time and initiate the law of scarcity. The producers of The Secret talk about how throughout the ages that The Secret, the Law of Attraction has been used by anyone who created anything substantial, but they kept it from you. They keep you on your toes anticipating the release of the movie, they limit the distribution, they create a new version of time relative to attracting.

- Practice "love bombing". The Law of Attractionists shower people with love, they accept them, love them, care about them because they share a belief. Some of the teachers go so far as to say that love is a magical word. They tell their followers often how much they love them.

- Withhold love. – When people question or don't believe, they withhold their love, separate them from the group, suggest that they need deeper indoctrination before they can be allowed back into the fold.

- Control their behavior – Law of Attractionists have a very strict code about how they have to think and act if they are to be able to manifest the things that they want. Shift the blame for ALL their problems back onto them. Make them responsible for their victimization. Tell them who is best to and who not to associate with.

- Make them paranoid of their own thought processes – If you think bad things, bad things will happen to you. Critical thinking and questioning are your old "patterns" trying to hold you back.

- Claim authority – Indicate that you've been given, discovered or received this esoteric knowledge that you can now pass on. Get artificial titles to add credibility to your arguments.

- Develop dependence – Make people feel that they are dependent on you for access to more or deeper knowledge. Do not allow people to think critically or independently. Reward group think. Create coaches and other leaders that can walk people through the process of learning how to behave and what to do when.

- Encourage separation from non-believers – Tell them the best thing they can do is cut off those negative people who don't believe. Those negative people and the non-believers are the ones that will impact your thoughts and keep you from getting more of what you want.

- Tell them they are victims of their uncontrollable programming – Demonstrate by focusing on their failures, their unattained dreams and their current dreams. Show them patterns that they repeat.

- Tell them if their thoughts are not in proper alignment something bad may happen to them – If they think about the wrong things, they may attract disease, bills, obesity. Make them fearful.

Oh, in addition to revealing how a cult seduces and conditions its members, I just laid out the marketing plan for The Secret. I also exposed many political and religious organizations in that description as well.

I want you to pay particular attention to the conversations you hear moving forward around The Secret, look at the structure of a cult above and ask yourself where the ideas that are being presented fall.

Without question The Secret became the marketing juggernaut that it has because the producer smartly chose people who have tremendous marketing experience and significant followings. The challenge with that is that it is hard to know who is riding the wave and who is not. I was just on a teleseminar a few nights back debating a teacher of the Law of Attraction (not someone from the movie) and he admitted that he prescribed to the idea that you should sell people what they want not what they need and that he was pitching the Law of Attraction because it is what people wanted right now.

Many people have suggested that we wrote this book and did the teleseminar that you can listen to at www.thetruthisthesecret.com because we were not selected to be in The Secret. But nothing could be further from the truth. If any one of us had been invited to be in the movie, knowing what it was and what they wanted to sell and knowing the beliefs of the person promoting it, we'd have declined for the very same reasons we are talking about it now. Contrary to what some people believe we are not doing this to ride the coat tails of the publicity being generated by presentation of the Law of Attraction, we simply chose to stand up and say something about it as the absurdity increased.

One of the challenges of cults is that they try and cover up their most bizarre beliefs with smoke screens like science or pop psychology in order to more easily attract members. In the case of the Law of Attraction, a new age belief, some of the more bizarre beliefs have been noted publicly and connected (incorrectly) to quantum physics. And here is the rub; quantum physics is hard to understand, even for those who devote their lives to studying and testing quantum theory. But when you take ideas like "everything is energy" and begin making arguments that sound well formed and use simple ideas (like attracts like) it makes the science seem simple and the idea exciting. After all, it sounds like it is being supported by science.

But no one really checks, no one tests and no one demands proof.

So one of my counter arguments is that if money is as easy to attract as a feather then give away the money to people who need it and are not as skilled with The Secret and attract more. If the universe really is your catalog as the teachers teach, then money is irrelevant.

But see that isn't true. Even the Law of Attraction teachers would have to reluctantly agree that giving away your money and possessions and then setting out to attract more might not be a wise course of action. Not wise unless of course you are taking out a loan or putting thousands of dollars on your credit card to learn how to attract more.

People are more susceptible to the ideas cults have to sell when they are in emotional flux or they are searching for answers.

Americans in particular have been impacted by 9/11, a war, rapidly changing lifestyles due to economic conditions, outsourcing and many other sociological changes that we've experienced lately.

We are in a state of change, we want something different, we want something easy to get our heads around. Life isn't as simple as it was fifty years ago.

So we search.

The idea that you can be in control of your life, your destiny just by thinking; that you can create the things that you need with your thoughts sounds good. So you set out to manifest your perfect life and something happens.

Nothing.

You try; others around you are apparently manifesting whatever they want. Yet you still struggle.

So you ask the leaders and they tell you that you need more skills; that you need to surround yourself with people who are believers like you, you need to get filled up. And, you need to separate yourself from those people who don't believe; they'll pull you down, they'll keep you in your old way of thinking.

They invite you to a seminar. Of course you need to make an investment because money has energy and you have to spend it to get more. If you try and hold onto it you are exhibiting a lack mentality.

So you go to the event, you get high for a while, you feel so enlightened, you buy more courses and books, you identify.

And you start to scour the horizon for any example of something you thought coming into being. You look for correlations that can be drawn and you justify the teaching because justifying means you believe and if you believe it enough, you'll be rewarded just like you were taught.

And that is where they set the hook and pull you in deeper.

Except you aren't attracting, you are just becoming good at seeing correlations, the same ones that always existed.

The next step is to offer you opportunities to assist or volunteer. If you want to be around the process more and more so you can truly align yourself with the teachings, just show up and help out, you won't have to pay for the expensive seminar, you get to be there for free if you'll just help (and pay your way).

You are now moving into the inner circle. People know you, you are adored and loved for your willingness to help and be a part. And, you are seen as someone on the inside, someone who has a different level of connection to the leaders and teachers, they must have seen something in you, you are a minor celebrity yourself.

And still, you can't manifest things the way they say you should. But you are stuck.

Now, the others in the community are telling you stories of their success and you begin to tell them about the connections you made and all of the things you are working on manifesting that are sure to come to fruition. You develop friendships and relationships.

And the hook digs in deeper.

And now you can't question because if you question, you'll be scorned and so instead of questioning you begin to blame . . . yourself. You didn't believe enough, your thoughts were not pure enough, you focused on the wrong things. You have a belief that you are not aware of that is attracting the negative or worse, nothing at all to you.

And the cycle continues.

175

If you question or try to leave, the leaders or more likely your friends and like believers will pull you back in. Hope is around the corner, it is just one course away. Enlightenment is never easy, you have to work hard, dedicate yourself and spend more money.

The only people who consistently manifest anything are the gurus, the teachers. Because they have special skills, skills you don't have.

They have advanced communication skills. They know the truth; they know that without you they don't exist. They know that they have to get you to intensify your desire for salvation so that you won't waiver in your faith or commitment.

They encourage your separateness and your "uniqueness". They reinforce that you get it, that you are unique and that you must keep the faith no matter what. You are just a thought away from everything you want.

Recently someone who was angered about some of my observations about the Law of Attraction asserted that we were only one thought away from ending poverty, starvation, war and disease and all it will take is the right thought.

My response to him was simple.

Please think the thought or ask one of the other Law of Attraction experts to think it.

Use the Law of Attraction for good.

Interestingly the conversation stopped there, he didn't continue. Not surprising, but unfortunate.

See the problem really isn't just the Law of Attraction. The Law of Attraction is a starter belief, one that assumes there are many more you may not yet understand, but one powerful enough to get you to suspend disbelief or skepticism and in that state of suspension more ideas are inserted.

When disbelief is suspended people become very susceptible to believing anything is true.

Ask any magician.

But the beliefs go deeper and are potentially much more dangerous. The beliefs include ideas that we all "enter the world" with "patterns" that we have to live out unless we discover them and short circuit them by understanding and applying "the laws of the universe". This sounds a lot like the Calvinist doctrine of predestination that is taught in many Christian churches; the words "The Universe" are a simple substitution for "God".

Other dangerous ideas are those that focus around curing diseases including cancer, alcoholism and drug abuse to mention just a few. For example, Bob Proctor said on *ABC News* that if your body is in a healthy vibration disease can't stay there. He doesn't bother to reveal how you test for a healthy vibration or what to do to achieve it. And even though he says that you should take traditional treatment if necessary, the implication is clear that if you think it, you'll get better.

When believers create new religions or ideas out of thin air as the New Age movement and the Law of Attraction has, there is even more room for manipulation of seekers. You simply make up more "laws" to support why someone is not attracting or manifesting what they want. These laws are arbitrary, made up by the purveyors of The Secret. And, there is no end to the laws that one can create to support why people are not manifesting or to create new streams of revenue.

The idea of the Law of Attraction becomes more attractive when there is the appearance that a miracle occurred. A drug addict reads a book or watches The Secret and stops using drugs and attributes it to the Law of Attraction-- they attracted their cure. They become poster children that the purveyors trot out as a demonstration of what you can become.

As the spiral continues more and more people get pulled in deeper and deeper, they think less and less and believe more and more. Unrelenting and unquestioning faith is valued at a much higher level than thinking and questioning. The basis for the irrational belief is no longer questioned.

Will more and more radical ideas and beliefs pop up out of this cult that following the Law of Attraction has developed? Absolutely.

The groups will continue to get more and more sophisticated in their stories, they'll come up with better and more credible sources and they'll attach themselves to The Secret with their beliefs in an attempt to grab market share and share in the wallet.

At the end of the day, cults can be good or bad.

And I come back to the original question: is the Law of Attraction a dangerous destructive cult?

And my answer remains the same . . . it depends.

And it depends on the extent to which the followers allow their critical thinking and will to take action to be subverted.

The good news is that pop psychology and trendy ideas tend to have a short lifespan in the United States and it is my belief that the Law of Attraction will too. It will follow an arc as other fads have in the past and then the next idea of the day will take its place.

Chapter Thirteen
Thinking About The Invisible
(BB)

The Secret is about invisible things like spirits, coincidence, the interconnection between thought and action and feeling and outcome, and the relationship between the physical universe and our psyche. It is a very tough and complex reality to deal with the invisible.

In the 17th century, in Salem, Massachusetts, some women were acting oddly and manifested certain peculiar bodily and emotional reactions. They had convulsions, exhibited weird body marks, and wept a lot. What was the explanation for their behavior? Back then, the invisible explanation for their behavior was that the women were witches, possessed of the Devil, and consequently, they were burned at the stake by the religious leaders of the day.

Nowadays, we might think they had epilepsy or hysterical personality disorder.

A few years ago a madman broke into a Bible study at a Dallas area church and he started shooting his gun. A few Christians were killed, a few injured, and yet one woman escaped serious injury when a bullet grazed above her head and only went through her hair. At the scene, when interviewed by a reporter, the husband of the "lucky" woman said that the Holy Spirit had guided the bullet and saved his wife's life.

No explanation was given as to why the Holy Spirit didn't redirect the other bullets.

A lot of people might think the more obvious explanation is that the bullets all followed their natural trajectories and it so happened that the woman's hair was the only thing in the way. Other people, not so lucky, had more than hair in the way.

These examples show how greatly our explanations about the invisible depend on our assumptions, our worldviews, or our philosophical or religious outlooks.

But the distance is also shaped by experience, ability to reason, personal and social history, and emotion. All manner of things come to bear when we deal with the invisible.

The extent of this is not easily grasped because very few people have a wide experience in the global village of our world. Despite the Internet, people's explanations tend to go in the direction of their local viewpoints and resident assumptions. If you were raised as a Buddhist in India or a Catholic in Italy, these religions and local cultures will be more than likely the source of your deepest beliefs. Therefore, one of the good things that can happen because of the dialogue about the Law of Attraction is that people can discover the uniqueness and "oddness" of their own views.

When we truly hear another person's experience and beliefs, it is parallel to what happens to us when we travel abroad. It is shocking to see that "not everybody does it our way" when it comes to almost every facet of life. And so a Catholic might be alarmed by the story of the spirit entity Abraham that was supposedly channeled by Esther Hicks. I am sure that Richard Dawkins or Sam Harris (two famous atheists) would be even more alarmed given their conviction that the supernatural is a wrong headed explanation for anything.

However, the Catholic can use his or her alarm to wonder: what is the difference between Abraham speaking from another realm to Esther, and the Judaeo-Christian belief that God spoke to the world through Moses and Isaiah and the archangel Gabriel and all the other people of the Bible? An atheist might find the book of Revelation to be nuttier than *The Law of Attraction* by Jerry and Esther Hicks.

The more we travel in the world of invisible explanations the more options become available. It is confusing, eye opening, and scary. Many may prefer not to travel.

We have shown you that a lot of people, including the writers of this book, do not appreciate the stark and frank blaming of victims that is a consequence of the unquestioning belief in Law of Attraction. And this does show the difficulty in dealing with something invisible, as in "we unconsciously attract negativity to our lives". Since you cannot see someone's unconscious, how can such a belief be either proved or disproved?

And what if the same blaming viewpoint was said from a Buddhist perspective, that a little girl raped in Darfur is being punished because she was a prostitute in a prior lifetime? That can't be proven or disproved either. But would we have been easier on it since it is coming out of a popular and ancient world wide religion rather than from a just-in-town new age TV producer from Australia?

That would be odd, too—and would illustrate the logical error called "genetic fallacy" where we rate a viewpoint based on where it comes from: i.e. we'll tread more softly if an idea emanates from Buddhism than from the Hicks' or Rhonda Byrne.

However, what makes evaluating The Secret very different altogether is that its followers have called their Law of Attraction a scientific law. If that is the case, then their viewpoints are subject to the rigors of the scientific method. And the scientific method reminds us of another important factor in relation to the invisible. What science depends on more than anything is a tracing of the visible and a finding of the visible to verify its hypotheses and laws and facts.

And here we remind ourselves that it has been a long, slow climb to discover penicillin and bacteria and trans fats and atoms and cells and diseases of the liver that are not merely explained by our moods. Therefore, it is disheartening to any scientist to read about the easy tossing away of what science has worked so hard to establish—e.g. how we gain or lose weight.

The "research" and "findings" in The Secret would be also dismaying for the serious scholar of religion, history, philosophy or English literature. Scholars in these fields would not think that the followers of The Secret had traveled with their eyes open to what Shakespeare or Einstein or Emerson or Churchill really believed. And most serious students of religion have not thought that the world is as loose and as cluttered with miracles as 21st century devotees of the supernatural seem to imagine.

In this sense, mankind has grown as it has tended to offer the simple explanation, the visible explanation, and if the supernatural was offered as an explanation it has been accompanied by more awe and wonder than seems to be evoked in the atmosphere of current thought.

Chapter Fourteen
Ask, Seek and Believe: What Does A Minister Say About The Secret?
(BB)

I do not find it easy to be a Christian. Though I was raised as a fundamentalist and spent 25 years as a Protestant minister, I still think:

A lot of the time it is difficult to be a Christian because we don't always want to forgive, be kind when someone hurts us, or give 10% to charity.

There are some Bible verses that we would not want said at our daughter's wedding.

King David makes Tony Soprano look like a saint.

The whole notion of eternal Hell is a bit troubling and certainly dangerous material when in human hands

Some Christians are very small-minded and even the best ones (Mother Teresa) are equaled by people of other faiths (the Dalai Lama) or no faith at all, when it comes to what really matters— human kindness.

However, there are aspects of Christianity and its history that illumine our thinking about The Secret. The Secret did not blow me out of the bathwater or make me enraged. I've heard it all before in the Christian world in which I grew up. I was trained to expect miracles, have faith that will move mountains and pray the prayer that will heal the sick. And this is expected of a Pastor. It's "Biblical" as long as it's Christ-Centered.

Here is what it's like to be a Pastor in the trenches.

I was a young Pastor, full of faith, Biblical knowledge, and awareness of my pastoral duties. A middle age woman in my parish contracted cancer of the spine. She was a nurse and knew this was not good news. But she kept coming to church worship, prayer meeting, and Deacon's meetings because she was a faithful, wonderfully kind Christian woman. I remember her smile to this day.

The whole church prayed for her, the whole town prayed for her— God, she had an 8 year old son, I bet even the town atheist secretly said something on her behalf. We even called a meeting of the whole church on a special night just to pray for her—and that got more people out than when I invited Dr. Bernie Siegel to speak at a special service.

But she ended up in the nursing home, bed-ridden because of her pain and decomposing spine. Her face and body ballooned up because of the "meds" and I dutifully visited her every week to say hi, tell her I love her, and pray for her healing.

Until one day, in the middle of the prayer, she gently grabbed my arm and said, "Bob, no more— let's face facts, God isn't going to heal me, so pray for me to die quickly and peacefully so this will be over."

If Fred Buechner is right that religion is a lump in the throat, well, I got religion that day.

Guess what? This story happens a million, million times a year in the presence of Pentecostal pastors who really believe in faith healing, in the presence of famous faith healers, in the presence of Christians untainted by diversity and philosophy, and in the presence of people without any faith who hope faith and healing will show up at the last minute.

Do you think a woman with spinal cancer doesn't really want to get better? Does she really want to attract more cancer in her spine?

If you think so, you be the one to tell her.

But see….here's the secret. When you are a long-term minister or a long-term psychotherapist, or a long-term friend, **your audience comes back every week.** And they are looking you straight in the eye, and expecting answers.

This is very different from the world of gurus who are alone with their disciples and with their theories. This is the opposite of a new age speaker who gives a fabulous, touching, totally certain and amazingly uplifting speech to a room filled with people who crave a trumpet's call. But the show moves on to the next town and the speaker does not have to deal with Wednesday's question, Thursday's doubt or Friday's agony.

The absent are easily out-argued and the exceptions are not invited for dinner.

Another story: I met a woman, a guest of friends, at an after-church luncheon. The woman was a very faith-filled believer whose daughter was struggling with cancer. Here was our brief conversation:

Me: "It's nice to meet you. We've been praying for your daughter and I hope she gets better."

Woman: (Looking intently at me and grabbing my arm): "Oh no, we don't hope she is going to get better, we *know* she is going to get better".
Me: "Well, it's great for your daughter that she has such loving and faith-filled parents."

She looks like such a believer and I look like doubting Thomas.

Alas, in less than a month the daughter was dead.

Did the mother change her viewpoint? I do not know. I never saw her again. But I doubt that she did because human beings can put up with a mountain of cognitive dissonance. This is the quiet alarm that goes off in your brain when you think those rare words: I might be mistaken.

It would have been ill timed of me to tell her about the mountain of unanswered prayers that have been sent out to the God of love who is revered more than the attraction-oriented universe.

It probably would not have worked anyway. People are seldom changed by a direct shot across the bow of the ship. When people are a million miles away from our viewpoint, there is too much distance between our "truth" and their "truth". Cognitive dissonance is bridged by proximity and repetition and a gradual opening of the mind. Otherwise, you have to use force and all that does is make slaves and prisoners.

And it is cruel to pull the carpet out from under someone's feet. You have to say: "Excuse me, could you please step to the side, this carpet is on fire."

And, even if the carpet is on fire, what if it is the dear priceless rug their children played on? It has been handed down by generations, with many stories woven into its heartfelt place in the family.

Then the family will try to stomp out the fire, save the carpet, and maybe shoot the messenger.

It is the same with belief systems—only way more so! We are all as defensive as cornered raccoons because we adore our viewpoints, secrets, and beliefs. Further, it is one thing to love your carpet, but what if you have been told that the carpet in your living room was given to you by God, no other carpet exists, and you must seriously and faithfully defend against those who would introduce a "false carpet" into your life?

This is the dilemma of any viewpoint that claims to have a God-given answer. You are now **double-locked against any new truth**— your own internal security alarm has now been backed-up and fool proofed by the greatest security system known in human history: God.

If you've only seen the dear God-given family carpet, it is the answer to all your floor problems and the only rug in existence of such beauty and value!

But what if you walk in a bigger world?

The Bible is over 2,000 pages long, written across 3,000 years, by about 45 major writers.

And all of those people took a walk around the block. And it was not the same block. And so they saw war and famine and bloodshed and foreign people and children dying and sons being killed and daughters being raped as well as angels singing and bushes burning and people walking through the Red Sea and prophets doing a long overdue miracle and Jesus turning water into wine and Jesus dying on a Cross and appearing to the disciples after He was dead.

And out of that whole mix and mess the entire ensemble of voices is supposed to be heard. Not just the success stories. In fact, these people are so trained to remember their whole history that they would get a C- for advertising. If you doubt me, read Ecclesiastes which mostly sounds like it was written by an atheist and has the following startling teaching:

> *Just as the deer is caught by the*
> *hunter, and the bird is taken in a*
> *snare by the fowler, so man is caught*
> *at an evil time and*
> *Time and chance happen to all.*

> Ecclesiastes
> 9:11, 12

No marketer is going to write that as "copy". And, if you go to church or synagogue, when's the last time you heard a sermon on that reality-oriented text? I can see the marquee: This week's Sermon: "You Could Have It as Bad as a Trapped Bird or a Dead Deer Even if You Attend This House of Worship".

If you are a serious follower of the Bible you are supposed to read the whole thing. And the above verse is very different from the following words by Jesus that the advocates of The Secret really cherish:

> *Ask and it will be given you, seek and you will find, knock*
> *and it will be opened unto you. For every one who asks*
> *receives, and he who seeks finds, and to him who knocks it*
> *will be opened.*

Now if you are a really serious student of the Bible, you can be diligent and learn the original language in which those words were written. It is koine Greek. Even though I was a Pastor for 25 years I'm as bad at languages as I am at quantum physics so you will hear nothing from me about physics and only this one thing about

Greek. **The tense of "ask" and "seek" and "knock" is in the aorist tense which means the verb tense connotes ongoing, unending action as in "always keep asking, always keep seeking and always keep knocking".**

So much for instant solutions.

The other vitally interesting aspect to the above verse is that it is taken from The Sermon on the Mount, which also has the following verses in it:

> *Beware of false prophets who come to you in sheep's clothing but inwardly are ravenous wolves.*
> *The gate is narrow and the way is hard that leads to life.*
> *Love your enemies.*
> *Deliver us from evil*
> *Our Father in heaven makes his sun rise on the evil and on the good, and sends rain on the just and the unjust.*

The above clearly teach that life can never be as easy as The Secret states, even if it *seems* implied by the "ask, seek and knock" of Jesus.

And Jesus knew that it was way worse than that, "we attract everything to us in a magnetic way". We have real enemies who come at us out of their own isolated, insular evil—otherwise, He would not have said to His enemies: "For which of the good works I have done, are you going to stone me?"

And in Jesus' worldview, God is far more gracious than one who would divvy up the world in a "you get what you attracted" kind of way. The sun shines on all out of God's generosity, not because we deserve or earn it or have sent out signals to the sun. If you are in the Sahara the sun is going to shine on you whether you want it to or not. The sun shines because it shines, the rain falls because it falls—you have nothing to do with it. This is certainly Jesus' view.

Of course this is where you can't out argue The Secret because they'll just say, "the reason the sun is shining on you is because you were afraid you'd have a heat stroke and so you attracted the sun to you."

Another thing that Jesus taught is that there are no thoroughly good people and no thoroughly bad people. In fact, inside each person and human system (church, family, business, government) is such an inter-mingling of good and evil that only on Judgment day can the whole mess be untangled. And, in every one of Jesus' parables about judgment, there is always a surprise in store. In the parable about the Good Samaritan it is he who is the moral hero, not the priest or rabbi, as would have been expected.

Given such complexity, how do thinking people embrace faith and reality? How do people who have their eyes open, still pray? Isn't that colluding with craziness and feeding into apparent craziness and the wild-eyed fanatics who sell their certainties?

Isn't prayer about as effective as gambling? The odds are not in your favor and the house seems to award the really skilled and the really lucky. (Note the parallel with attraction thinking. Just as the supposedly truly faith-filled believer will be healed, so the person skilled at the Law of Attraction will attract positive things.)

I believe miracles happen. They are not a guarantee that all things will be well in this instant, but that down the road "all things shall be well and all manner of things shall be well". So, prayer is hope in action and it expresses love and concern—and I do worse things on a regular basis.

Likewise, people will follow The Secret and attempt to attract things. They too could do worse.

There is another thing that is at work in phenomena such as religion and the movement based upon the Law of Attraction. Their adherents are "in love"—in love with their God, answer, theory and success. Therefore, they speak in the language of love, which is often the language of exclusion (I love no one else but you), hyperbole (with you in my life everything will be terrific), and passion (you are so terrific for me, there's no need for anything else).

And so when Jesus talked about "ask, seek and knock" he wasn't giving a scientific or philosophical treatise. He was imploring people in a wild, wake-up way to start doing something about their lives. He is fighting a common human flaw where we sit back, do nothing, and hope others will take care of us. In the psychotherapy world, this is called "passive-dependent personality disorder".

It's like you have to read the fine print—and think and think and think. Is this a poem? Is this meant literally? Is this hyperbole? Is this a cliché? Does this cliché cover everything? If the world were as simple as our clichés, the Bible would be a very thin book. It is not a very thin book.

And the Bible would be even longer if it had all the answers or was as long-winded as Abraham—the spirit entity from the other world channeled through Esther Hicks. In the Bible you seldom see behind the curtain. There is awareness of the immense silence of God, the predominance of evil, the brokenness of people (it's not a level playing field in the Bible—the poor are assumed to need extra help, not just a magnetic heart to attract what they need), and the fact that there is "a great gulf fixed" between this world and the next. The mysteries are noted and believed in and felt—but we do not get the HTML text and the video replay and the philosophy notes to explain anywhere near everything.

In this sense, the Bible is not a marketing text, the *National Enquirer*, a 30 second sound byte, or the *National Geographic*. Its basic tenet is: "The secret things belong to God" and you better pay most attention to what is right before your eyes—the next duty, the poor man in the ditch, the loser who might be Jesus disguised as "the least of these my brethren".

And, in the Bible if any secret is conveyed or any angel seen, there is usually such a sense of awestruck wonder and humility on the part of the human recipient that your choices are basically that the person is either crazy or that they had a brush with God. It doesn't sound like the legion of chatty narcissists who confuse their thoughts and opinions and feelings with God.

Is there any religious person who has ever uttered the words from St. Paul: "I do not have a word from the Lord on this."

I once heard a learned professor speak about Christianity as he gave the Lyman Beecher lectures on preaching at Yale. He said something I've never forgotten: "What people really believe in is their daily lives." What saturates our soul every day is what we are surrounded by and I imagine that gurus on The Secret are not surrounded by the truly broken, the retarded, the psychotics, the manic depressives, the stupid, the scared, the really scared, and the people with no marketable skill.

The writers of the Bible knew that life could be a mess. You can hear the cries of people in the Bible. There is no crying in The Secret. Life is an attract-it picnic in The Secret.

This leads us into our next chapter where we will examine the view of people conveyed in the Secret.

Chapter Fifteen
What Does A Psychotherapist Say About the Secret?
(BB)

The world's best and brightest have serious blind spots, lots of defense mechanisms, a lousy ability at arguing, and at least one major character defect. Even the best and brightest need more than their own inner ability to attract something.

I have also seen people who are not the world's best and brightest. Some people's souls are like what a body looks like when there's been a head-on collision. They are fragmented, beat up, ripped apart, and filled with a near deadness that some will never understand. Some people are so backed away from life that they can virtually attract nothing because they are so distanced from any magnet.

And they are paranoid (afraid of any magnet), borderline (certain the magnet is undependable), obsessive (line up everything before the magnet arrives), hysterical (crying so loud you drown out the frequency of the magnet), depressed (feeling there is no magnet), anxious (there might be a magnet and a better carpet, but my soul is on fire), or just plain neurotic like the rest of us.

The path to wholeness is **a long battle for all**. It is a long, long battle for the truly broken. And that is the real reason why we want the quick fix. We constantly try to avoid the long battle.

We don't have the love or the time or the money to help others and ourselves. Above all, we don't have the patience (here's about the only other Greek fact I remember from Seminary—the Greek word for patience combines two words, one which means "long" and the other which means "passion". Patience is "long passion").

In one respect, I agree with the Secret: we all do need to practice gratitude and positive thinking—including those who have little to be thankful for as they shovel for food in a Bangladesh dump. Above all, taking the next step of action towards a better life is what needs to be accomplished—but for some 8 year old girls in Bangkok that means sleeping with American tourists to obtain money for their families back home in the village.

If you wonder for 5 minutes what that does to the soul of an 8 year old girl, you will know this secret: none of us **can walk 10 feet in the shoes of the people we all so easily blame**.

Let's face it: for all kinds of reasons, even the best of us are pretty miserable at steadily, lovingly, and brilliantly seeing the heart and world of the other.

We are too forgetful, self-absorbed, tired, angry, and filled with stereotypes that blind us to the reality of the other person.

Notice the word "blind". It's a strong word. A blind man cannot see. It is not a choice and I imagine he does not want it.

Here's the very painful not obvious truth: we are all emotionally blind. We all do not see.

Here's an example. I have been present at many a conversation where a group of wealthy people nod their heads with vigorous consent when one of them says, "I just can't imagine how anyone can't make tons of money. It's so easy."

Do we have to go back to the 8 year old in Bangkok? No, let's not go there.

Instead, picture an ensemble of very talented, classical pianists or a group of top-notch parachutists or a troupe of people from Cirque de Soleil (are they even the same species?). All of them can sit around their campfire and casually say, "I just can't imagine why anyone can't play Mozart or jump out of a plane or trapeze in the air. It's so easy."

Here's another example: how often have we heard it said that if we took all the money away from Bill Gates or Larry Ellis or Warren Buffet they would have it back in 10 years? Guaranteed. And especially guaranteed if they know the Secret.

True? Maybe. Maybe not. Does Bill Gates have another Microsoft in him and would IBM accept it this time? What if Larry Ellis is taken to a dictatorship where all the money goes to the dictator? What if terrorists wreak the havoc we fear? Will Warren Buffet do as well in the Stock Market? Will it exist?

Can any of these men learn Cirque de Soleil? I hope they are very good at attraction.

Very talented people tend to forget **how hard it is to get to their level**. All of the untalented might want to forget that, too— because then we can search for the quick fix and ignore our despair, confusion, mediocrity, laziness, and lack of patience to climb any ladder of success.

Most of all, every one who writes a book or an article seems to forget how sheer luck is a very big factor in existence. We forget because that messes up our simple theories and our tidy answers and our cozy conversations.

But let's think again of the really broken. Let's say your so-called stupidity has been pointed out to you 16,000 times by your father and mother. Not once do they notice your brilliance because they are lost in their own world. Instead, you hide under the covers in

197

your bed because you are told you are stupid, stupid, stupid. You don't even notice that, silently, you have always out argued your parents because, actually, you are way smarter than they are.

One day your 4th grade teacher teaches you to play chess and you beat him in one month. Everyone realizes how smart you are, but given how beat down you are it is only a slight hint to you. It is snuffed out by your parent's attitude that night. In grade 9 you beat the best chess player in school. And your favorite uncle says those magical words, "Gosh, I always knew you were smart, but not this smart."

The emotional cataracts come off and you begin to see....but it takes as much "practice, practice, practice" to erase the damage and walk in emotional truth as it takes to be a Cirque de Soleil acrobat. And even they slip from time to time.

The Law of Attraction states that your negative vibes attract and increase the abuse.

Is my psychological description the same as the attraction process in The Secret? No....because this has *no* blame towards you at all. It blames the enemy totally.

This does not assume you are attracting the accusation that you are stupid even though you are three years old.

Emotional growth is not easy. The Secret implies that it is quick and that it is available for everyone.

It is a lot easier to believe The Secret than to face the amazing injustice in the world, the unfairness of life, the brokenness of people, the sheer power of luck, and the long climb to human wholeness.

How did we come to stray so far from obvious truth? How can it be that America (the land of "liberty and justice for all") has become a breeding ground for blame of the highest proportion? I am not a sociologist so I will only mention the following sources: the brief attention span created by television; the materialism which does not foster deep soul understanding; the sense of entitlement bred into our current generation. Overall, our culture demands a quick fix.

But I do want to share some further illumination from the psychotherapy world I have worked in for 20 years. When people are having difficulty on the long climb to human wholeness, these are the words they will inevitability hear:

"You do not want to change."

This is what a faith healer will say to a still sick person. It is what a TV host will say to his guests. It is what the advocates of The Secret will say to people who do not attract good things their way. Deep down, you did not want the _____.

We can look at this in two ways. First of all, ask a million people and they will say they have experienced the fact that they wanted something with total passion and did not get it. When I was a kid I had a bone disease. I remember at age 10 lying in a ditch with a mailbox on my shoulder and a bicycle over the rest of my body. With utter purity I wanted one thing—no broken bone. In my little heart I asked for that one thing to what I thought was the best part of the Universe. An hour later I got my answer—an X-ray that showed a broken clavicle. Accidents abound in this universe, as do the hearts that do not want them.

But anyone can sit in an office, far from the ditches of the world, far from the hearts of the world, shake his or her head and solemnly announce: "There are no accidents."

199

We can also come at this from a different direction. Let's examine the phrase "I do not want to" and "I want to" and we will begin with watermelon.

Do you like watermelon? You do, so do I—so let's simply say together:

I want watermelon.

Do you like lima beans? No, neither do I—so let's simply say together:

I do not want lima beans.

That seems rather simple. But what if I told you that all the research has shown that watermelons are bad for your heart and lima beans will cure hardening of the arteries?

I'm 53, with a healthy heart and so I will say, "I don't want lima beans but I will eat a few now and then…and I will have watermelon now and then because I so enjoy the taste."

But what if you are 73 and have significant hardening of the arteries? You might say, "No more watermelon and bring on the lima beans."

So, it is getting a bit more complex. Already you can see that there is a different "I" and a different sense of "want" as we go through this watermelon want journey.

On that journey, reality changes again and we are told that watermelons are a vital part of the sacred meal to be shared at your son's wedding. He married someone from one of the Caribbean islands where they are "into" watermelon in a big way. And I've been told that my daughter's wedding features lima beans mixed with the best pot in the world. Should I want lima beans mixed with marijuana?

You will reluctantly "want" to eat the watermelon to keep your son happy and I will reluctantly eat the lima beans with marijuana to please my daughter. You will be worried about your heart and I will wonder what people think of me with my lima-pot mixture.

Now, what if we have to climb a 14,000 foot mountain to obtain the watermelon for your son's wedding and the lima beans and pot for my daughter's? And what if you who are 73 are really out of shape and I at 53 am on crutches? Could we then simply say, "I do not want watermelon" and "I do not want lima beans"?

See how the words "I" and "want" have actually changed. Initially, "I want watermelon" was simple and clear and easy in that a cohesive, single-minded "I" wanted an easily obtainable object (a nice juicy watermelon). By the end, the "I" is physically hurt, ambivalent (watermelon is bad for me, but I love the taste), and tired (14,000 feet uphill is a long way to go for watermelons or lima beans). By the end, the lima beans have gone from a disgusting tasting object to a necessary nutritional item to a companion to a high.

This is all to show you how complex it is when we say, "I want something." But do you think this enters our minds when we blame others? No, we're in too much of a hurry for that kind of thinking and soul exploration.

So defenders of The Secret will say I did not want to attract a healthy collarbone, as the rest of us will so casually and quickly say:

He does not want to stop drinking.
She does not want to lose weight.
He does not want to control his spending.

She wants to keep her abusive husband.
He does not want to listen to correction.

And it is all nice and simple, as in:

I want watermelon and
I do not want lima beans.

And, as long as we think in this quick fix way, we will never notice that "just" is the dirtiest word in the English language ("just say no"), and that nothing is easy until you've done it a thousand times. Nor will we have to notice people's IQ and the difference that makes to the "I". And, above all, we won't have to lend a long listening ear to a friend who cannot leave her abusive husband.

So, let's say you go over to your friend's house and discover that her husband got drunk, knocked over her furniture, and beat her for the tenth time this year. In case my watermelon example did not convince you to the folly of simply saying, "she does not want to change", let's compare your soul and hers, her life and yours.

You live with a kind, patient husband who has affirmed you in a variety of ways for ten years. He has only slightly raised his voice at you all those years. You come from a family that supported you with love, material comfort and a fine education. They also encouraged you to continual growth, self-respecting behavior, and offered the occasional firm reminder. You have $750,000 in a retirement account and $600,000 in savings. You have lots of friends and relatives who think you are wonderful. And you are supported by the community of folks you have come to know at the local Episcopal Church.

You are "lucky". Your "I" is quite strong and when you say, "I want" something your "want" is single-minded, passionate and confident. There is little fear in your soul as you start a new project.

Your friend lives with a brute that has found a variety of ways to crush her soul. He has yelled at her every day for ten years. Her family is on the opposite side of the country, but they never ever did much for her anyway—because her father was crippled with arthritis and the mother worked as a waitress at the local diner to support the four kids and her husband. So, there wasn't much attention to go around and when the mother came home she yelled a lot because life was overwhelming.

College was out of the question for your friend and the first excitement of her life was when Johnny, her husband, took her out West in his big semi and promised to settle down in California and raise a family. They have $5000 in a retirement account and $800 in savings. You are her only friend. She goes to a local charismatic church that promises a "claim it" sort of faith backed up by great Gospel singing. She finds your church to be rather boring.

Her "I" is not the same as your "I" because hers is fragmented, filled with despair, and confused. And when she wants something the "want" is a very tiny force compared to the drums of fear that beat in her soul. Her "I" is "a mist driven by a storm" (St. Peter).

If your friend decided to go to therapy, she might easily be viewed by the therapist as dependent, because she would need two sessions a week. That would be a huge mistake on the therapist's part, because your friend is not dependent at all. She never had anything to depend on. In my professional opinion, you are the dependent one because your soul has been supported and strengthened by a thousand people. Your friend lives on a shoestring in every way.

Of course she wants to change and leave her husband in the easy, "I want a watermelon" kind of way. But in her life the watermelon has been poisoned, her jaw has been broken, there's no money for even lima beans, and her husband told her if she buys another watermelon (i.e., she leaves) he is going to have sex with their daughter when he has her on the weekend.

If this still does not convince you of **the lunacy of our quick-fix, claim it, attract it, easy-riddled, just let it go, don't take it personally, don't let things get to you beliefs**, then let me inform you finally of what thoughts, passions, wants and beliefs really are.

A thought is not merely an idea. It is lightening that can strike terror at the heart of a soul as in the night that a little girl knew she was not safe with her father. Or it is a ray of sunshine like the day when you knew you were smart.

A passion is not a passing moment. It is a hurricane that can sweep away everything in your life. Or it is a hot front coming from the west that gives you a new dream.

A want is not a fleeting brain wave. It is a hill that you have to climb because you want to see the other side.

A belief is not a page in a book that you tear out on a whim. A belief is the Mt. Everest that sits in your soul like a 29,000 foot huge rock.

Each of us, in our own unique way, is a combination of Mt Everest, hills, hurricanes, a pleasant hot front, lightening bolts and rays of sunshine.

Last time I checked it was not easy to climb Mt. Everest or manage lightning or redirect a hurricane. And often those who have to climb Mt. Everest have had few hills to practice on, little sunshine, and infrequent breaks from any weather.

If this is too grim or too hard to accept, you can take the easy route and just say:

"People in trouble don't want to change. If only they wanted to attract better things."

And you will have a whole chorus to join you because **The Secret is the last frontier so far discovered in our endless search for a quick fix world!**

A final point.

If anything like the Secret were true, Shakespeare need not have taken the immense trouble to teach us about family strife as in Hamlet or jealousy as in Othello; he could merely have felt the need for peace in his soul and emitted it to 17th century England. Likewise there would be no need for Churchill's speeches and British sons dying on the shores of Normandy—they all could have magnetically begun to attract peace. And Plato could have had Socrates sit down and do some attraction thinking (it's far easier than Socratic dialogue).

The Secret casts a blind eye to all the people helping the paralyzed whose spinal cord is *totally* severed (including, say, a professional football player who reached the top of his game using visualization and asking and believing, but those mental games don't repair severed nerves). It sends a subtle mockery to all the volunteers working in mental health clinics to encourage the crushed soul who has 1 ounce of hope and 262 lbs. of despair. It rebukes all the government people filling out forms for the disenfranchised to get food stamps and subsidized housing.

The Secret is a mockery of all novels and self-help books. If the Secret is totally true, our books and forms need only be one sentence long:

"Really soulfully wish for what you are lacking and it will begin to appear."

If that is true, then of course we wasted our time writing this book. We could have just wished for the clarity and charity to show up on everyone's doorstep.

Chapter Sixteen
Exploring And Getting The Edge
(DL)

I've said it often, I'm an explorer.

I regularly put myself in the fray in front of others because I love the excitement and challenge of discovering new ideas and new frontiers. I also like disproving ideas to make room for even better and more important ideas.

Are my conclusions always correct? Of course not, but I find that when I practice sound thinking more often than not I find the truth quickly.

I'll never stop exploring and I hope you never will either.

I began studying metaphysics and positive thinking shortly after I left the cult that I was raised in. I've studied psychics, faith healers, tongue speakers, the Law of Attraction, mental magnetism, energy healing and much more.

Would you like to hear something surprising? I'd love for them to be real. I'm completely fascinated by the idea that I might be able to send some of my energy into another person and have them be healed. I'm enamored with the idea that if I have faith as a grain of a mustard seed that I could say to the mountain "remove hence to yonder place and it shall remove and nothing will be impossible to you." I love the idea that Yoda could have a tiny little bag of Jedi mind tricks that would allow him to control the minds of others.

207

But at the end of the day, none of it is real. Not only is there no scientific evidence when asked to perform one of these feats, the people who proclaim to be able to do them cannot.

For some people thinking about these ideas can provide stimulus to think about what might be, to dream bigger dreams and take more daring actions to achieve the things that are important to them in this life.

And to that extent I appreciate the idea of the Law of Attraction but at the end of the day there is no science to support it and in fact, the science tends not to support it and counters it's claims. It is simply a nicely packaged idea that is easy to buy right now.

And there will be another to follow it.

And here is the real difference when thinking about these things. Most people don't think.

But if you choose to explore, you must think, you must reason and you must base decisions on the best evidence that you have currently in order to move forward effectively. Imagine what would have happened to Lewis and Clark if they had floated down rivers having faith that they'd never run into massive rapids or waterfalls. Or what if they simply chose to attract food and supplies and not to have a mindset of fear and suspicion when entering unknown territory? If they'd have made those choices our history might be a lot different than it is today.

So will I continue to explore many of the ideas around success, mental power, faith, belief, and energy? The answer is yes but I'll do it using scientific skepticism, critical thinking and my starting point will always be the best scientific information we have today. So I'll explore in the way that Lewis and Clark did by stepping into unknown or uncharted territories and using the very best technology to help me draw my conclusions.

And, I'll maintain a malleable mind with a focus on testing what appears to be real or true. The moment that something like faith healing, Law of Attraction, spoon bending (beyond the magician's trick), telepathy, or speaking to long dead relatives can be proven and predictably replicated, then I'll become a believer and supporter.

Many people ask me the question, "If the Law of Attraction doesn't work, then what does? How do I give myself an edge?"

That is a very good question and many great books have been written to answer it. But I'll try and answer it here clearly and succinctly without writing another tome.

There are ways to give yourself an edge. The first is to study voraciously and to surround yourself with unique stimulus and ideas. But the trick is not to allow the emotional content of the idea to overwhelm your ability to step back and see where and how the idea fits and if it is real and true, or if it requires more testing and thinking.

Take someone "weird" to lunch and check out their worldview, see what they are thinking about and why . . . and overlay it on your own experience and see what changes. It is by becoming aware of the differences, the subtle changes and taking action on those items that can move you forward in a powerful new way.

The next way to give yourself an edge is to ignore the mass media's interpretation and opinions of the information at hand. Instead, be an investigator. When you hear something interesting, odd or offbeat make it your responsibility to look into it. Derive your own opinions from researching. Don't read just one article on the Internet and call it good. Do actual research. You'll be amazed at what you learn that you can use to either expand your experience . . . or stop doing and believing things that are inefficient.

Seeing an edge is about being incrementally better, about being incrementally faster and about being incrementally smarter. The difference between a dull knife that rips and a sharp knife that slices is an incrementally thinner edge.

Start asking the question, "why?" more often. My daughter is three years old as I write this and she loves to ask why. And, as an adult the quickest way to get me fired up is to respond to the question why with, "because I said so." That is not an appropriate answer to why. She is three; she doesn't have the language to ask better questions (though I'd argue that why is a VERY good question). Her question about why is her attempt to understand what is happening around her. Giving her good information now lays the groundwork for making better decisions later. But telling her, "because I said so" narrows her worldview and makes her stop exploring and thinking. I won't have that for her and I won't have it for you.

Asking why is a way of getting more information. One of my favorite questions to ask people is why they believe something. Try it out, it is amazingly eye opening. Ask someone today, "Why do you believe X?" Then, listen to their answer. Is their answer based on personal experience, research, thought, reasoning, the media interpretation or nothing at all? You'll often find that people really don't know why they believe what they believe and that is dangerous. It means that they are moving through life accepting information that is directed at them as being true without considering it at all. Their experience is, "It sounds good. Others are doing it so it must be true and good."

Another way of getting an edge is to say yes more often. In my forty odd years on this planet so far I've had far more experiences than people twice my age. Why? A big reason is because I said yes more often than they did. When I see an opportunity to explore, experience, study or research anything that is even remotely interesting to me more often than not I'll say yes.

And, when I say yes I dive in. I question, challenge, think, experience and form opinions. I don't just dip my toe in the water either. I don't read a book on the topic; I read twenty or thirty books on the topic. I read research papers, I pick up the phone and call the thought leaders in the area and ask them questions. I want to know what they think about and how they came to their conclusions. And I keep getting deeper and deeper into the experience to understand how it has application to me and my life . . . or if it does at all.

I want to encourage you to say yes more often with a qualification: say yes but don't accept what you see on the surface, particularly when it comes to ideas that are way out there.

I also abandon things quickly.

When things turn out to be untrue, uninteresting or unfulfilling I move on. If things can't be quantified and I can't figure out a way of measuring or quantifying them (when it matters) and the thing that I'm saying yes to isn't necessary to support life and existence I move on. It is a problem for someone else to solve who is more interested in it than I am. I abandon many more ideas than I keep.

When you abandon those things that are not useful it gives you an edge because you know one path that you won't be going down and you know one idea that doesn't fit in with your worldview.

The next way to give yourself an edge is to change your mind. Give yourself permission to revisit old ideas or beliefs, challenge them, find out of they are still (or ever were) true. In my experience I see people spending way too much time trying to make something be true that they had believed. Give yourself

211

permission to change your mind. Be malleable but don't be fooled. Master your emotions; temper them with reason and critical thinking. There is always room for emotional thinking in critical thinking but there is never room for critical thinking in bullshit.

Another big edge exercise is to travel internationally. International travel will open your eyes to many new ideas and opportunities. It will also open your eyes to the challenges that people in other countries face that you many never have faced in your lifetime. Sure you can see it on television, but it isn't the same as seeing, feeling, touching, tasting, and smelling first hand.

My brother told me an interesting story. When he was in his twenties, he wanted to see what it was like to be homeless so he drove to San Francisco and stayed with the homeless people there for a few days. He lived with them during the day and slept with them at night. He had a very real experience. I asked him what he learned from the experience and for him it was that homelessness was never an option and that he needed to deepen his relationship with his family. Now I'm not saying that you need to go to that extreme. My brother is a real explorer; he recently climbed the highest mountain in Idaho where we live. But once you put yourself in an experience you can never see it the same way again. And that experience and that difference will often times be the thing that sparks an idea that you can take action on that will make all the difference.

Many people will say, "I'd love to do that but I don't have the money." In the United States we are bordered by two very large countries that nearly anyone can get to. But even if you can't travel internationally, travel to a big city that has significant populations from other cultures-- go to a Chinatown or Little India. If you can't do that, strike up a friendship with an immigrant, ask them to share their experiences of their homeland. You'll be amazed at what you learn and think about when you get a completely different perspective. And, take a look at the beliefs that they have that got them where they are or that have kept their country from evolving.

The final way to give yourself an edge is to know that when you pay attention to something you'll find more connections, similarities, correlations and new ideas than ever before. When you set out with the intention of solving a problem, finding a solution, getting a new job, making more money or finding the cure for cancer you become more aware of the possibilities. Think of it this way, when you buy a new car you suddenly become aware of all the other cars like yours.

And this explains one of the reasons why the Law of Attraction seems to work for some people. They create a vision board and they set the intention that they'll get all of those things and sure enough they begin to get some of them. But it isn't that the universe is manifesting these things, it is that they are getting them or "creating" them because they took some action on the opportunities that always existed around them but that they didn't see until they started exploring the possibility. There is nothing magical about that, it is how all problems are solved – Identification, Attention, Focus, Action, Outcome, Reevaluate. That is the process for solving any problem or getting more of anything you want. And that may in fact be the ultimate edge.

Inattentional blindness is a malady that impacts all of us at one time or another. It was first discovered in factories where there were high repetitive motion injuries. But the way you've experienced it is this: You get into your car in the driveway to go to work, start it up, put it in reverse, back out, put it into drive and the next thing you are aware of is being at work and not remembering a thing that happened along the way. You were inattentionally blind to the things around you because you were so familiar with them. This is a real problem in jobs with a lot of repetitive action. People become inattentively blind and don't see the danger as it approaches them and are injured.

213

Many people go through their lives inattentionally blind. They hear something, accept it as being true because it sounded good, it got their adrenals flowing, the dopamine kicked in and it felt good . . . and so they repeat the process again and again without thinking about it or noticing what is going on around them.

But in that moment of becoming aware, of looking around, you begin to see the opportunities that were always around you silently (or not so silently) begging for you to take advantage of them.

John Cage wrote 4 minutes 33 seconds, considered by many a classical masterpiece. A musician comes on stage and sits down at a piano for 4 minutes and 33 seconds. Occasionally he'll turn the pages of the music in front of him or sip some water but other than that, nothing.

But what happens next is something very interesting. It would appear to most that it would be very quiet but in fact, something unique happens to everyone and for everyone. They become aware of what they were inattentionally blind to (or more accurately deaf to).

The audience becomes aware of the sounds in the silence around them. The shifting of seats, the breathing of the people around them, their own pulse or heart beats, the traffic, the fans. But what is unique about that? According to music reviewer Peter Gutman, the "silence" invites one's memories and gives rise to associations.

In that way, by studying, by thinking and by becoming aware of the silence around us we are able to make great associations and as a result solve more problems and get more of what we want.

Taking action connects the dots and the dots lead to whatever it is that you want if you take enough of the actions to get there.

Many of the ideas that we hold to be true are actually some form of old mythologies. I'd like to suggest something very important to you right now. I'd like you to spend a day or two exploring mythology and I'd like you to start by getting Joseph Campbell's book *The Hero with a Thousand Faces*. Read that book. Or if you prefer not to read, get the delightful DVD series done by Bill Moyer and Joseph Campbell called *Joseph Campbell and The Power of Myth*. This will be a very eye opening experience and allow you to make a lot of connections that you may have been inattentionally blind to as well.

If you really want to get more out of life, ask better questions and more clearly define what you want.

There is tremendous power in clarity. The more specific you can be about what you want the easier it is to achieve. However it isn't guaranteed. It doesn't matter how clear you are about wanting to be the world's richest person if you don't take all the proper actions (which will involve a fair amount of hard work) in the right order and aren't able to handle the ups and downs and maintain your focus as you continue forward.

One of the challenges that I often see with people who are seeking more from their life is that they set too many goals. In all likelihood you'll be lucky to accomplish one significant goal in a year. By significant I mean lose 10% of your bodyweight if you are overweight or increase your income by 10 – 20%. However, our temptation is to put down all the things that we want to accomplish in a year as goals and direct our focus on achieving all of them. The problem with that is that it fragments our focus and effort and so we actually accomplish less than we would if we simply focused on one thing at a time. Setting too many goals and then multitasking is actually a means of creating interruptions in our plan.

I wrote a whole book called *The Power of an Hour: Business and Life Mastery in One Hour a Week.* The premise of the book was: how do you change your life or your business in one hour a week? And the answer is fairly simple. Define what you want to achieve, gather your tools, remove distractions, create focus and go to work. Of course I give many ideas about how to focus and what to focus on to create fast results in certain areas of life or business, but the idea remains the same whatever it is that you want.

I'd like to encourage you to spend one hour a week exploring. Look at new ideas, expand your mind, go someplace you've never been and see what others are thinking about. Go to your local bookstore and read a magazine you'd never even considered reading before, go ahead, walk right up to the rack, close your eyes, and read through whatever magazine you pick up.

Then, think.

Once you've learned about something new, I want you to spend another hour during the week thinking about it. That's right, I want you to practice your thinking skills. I want you to use reasoning, logic, creative thinking, and narrowing down. I want you to draw a conclusion to create an opinion.

Then I want you to notice how good it feels.

The reason that ideas like the Law of Attraction get big so fast is that we lost the rich taste for thinking and replaced it with the fast food alternative of "that sounds good enough for now."

If "good enough for now" is not good enough for your life in general, then I want you to reengage your mind. I want you to experience what happens when you put real brainpower to work. You'll be stunned by how your life will change and how much simpler life becomes.

Life is about imagining, thinking but most importantly doing.

And, life on your own terms does not involve blindly accepting ideas that have no chance of being proven . . . even mine. Living life on your own terms means coming to your own educated, reasoned conclusions. Sometimes it means standing up to the masses and screaming, "Something is wrong here, open your eyes with me!"

Often, living life on your own terms means simply defining the kind of life that is comfortable and meaningful to you and not buying into the emotion and pressure of "having it all" as defined by others. Maybe having enough is enough.

And nearly always living life on your own terms involves giving something back to those less fortunate around you or solving some significant problem that will leave the world a little better place. As I get older I find myself exploring more of those areas of life than I ever did before and I find service to others to be endlessly fascinating.

And if I could wish a magical wish or think a positive thought and solve the problems of the world, I'd spend the rest of my life thinking those things. But until then I'm going to explore and take action.

I hope I meet you on my journey and I hope we collaborate in a life that is bigger than both of us.

And, I hope I've inspired you to think in ways you've never thought and explore in ways you've never explored.

But mostly, I hope that I've inspired you to take action.

Because that is The Secret!

Conclusion
The Real Magic
(BB)

The Secret got some of the real magic exactly right. To face the powerful obstacles of life (internal and external), we need to be positive, grateful, future-focused, expectant and looking for better opportunities. We need to want those opportunities as powerfully as a man with his head on fire wants water.

And part of the real magic of life is hearing enthusiastic, inspiring people. The Secret DVD had plenty of vitality in this regard.

But more magic is needed.....of varied kinds.

We do not want you to be overwhelmed by earth's catalog of HELP buttons, so we offer you, in summary, seven magical keys to success and well-being. They are magical in that they work and can lead to amazing results.

The first magic key is Enthusiasm. Most of us start off with great enthusiasm and fire in our bellies. If you do not have enthusiasm, we do not blame you. Undoubtedly, life has hurt you and you have hurt yourself and blamed yourself. So you do not need our blame. What you need is forgiveness, a sense of what you have already accomplished, and a renewed sense of the unique dream you want to pursue. This will build your enthusiasm.

Despite your fresh dream and enthusiasm, obstacles will come your way. The degree to which you plan for obstacles is a big start on the path to getting where you want to be. As Kevin Hogan says

219

in his CD programs, "Prepare for the worst, hope for the best." Your enthusiasm for the goal, the dream, and your new success has to be as big as the obstacles. Enthusiasm is the rocket blast to get you going.

The second magic key is Courage. The biggest inner obstacle you will face is fear. The gurus downplay this because they are almost always working in their comfort zone. If everyone who sold you something had to perform in Cirque de Soleil before they wrote their guarantees, they would be reminded of the power of fear and the reality of being a beginner. Then their guarantees would sound something like this:

> If you buy this book or CD we cannot guarantee very fast results because you may be handicapped by fear and it takes a massive amount of skill, luck and experience to succeed in the area we have spent a lifetime. It takes a lot of time and support to overcome fear and, frankly, we cannot give you that time or support. But please buy our product anyway.

It is not possible in the space of this book to teach you all you need to know in how to get through fear. It is the leading cause of any of us being "slow as molasses". The courage to move through fear is indispensable in the journey to success.

The third magic key is Endurance. Given the power of fear and other obstacles, you will need the following muscles to help you endure: preparation, planning, organizing, patience, practice and love. A good road map will save you so much trouble. Patience is needed for the long journey.

And we hope you have fallen in love with your new goal, project or dream because, as C.S. Lewis used to say, "The language of love is the language of eternity." When we love someone or something, it always is a forever phenomenon. Forever separates the true love from the overnight kind.

The days to come will show how much you truly loved your new project, goal, idea and dream to make your life better. If you need more staying power, focus on you whom you love and how your dream will make their lives better.

You will also need to receive love. If that is especially difficult for you, you may need the skill and acceptance of a fine therapist. (Did any one ever tell you that Freud said, "Psychotherapy is in essence a cure through love"?) Psychotherapy is the magic playground where you work through your fear that you are not loved. You will have to change the difficult things about you that may lead you to think you are not loved. You will discover that you are more messed up than you thought. You will also discover that you are more wonderful than you imagined.

Psychotherapy, at its best, is precise surgery for the soul. It is not a general platitude or an easy answer as The Secret proposes. In the hands of a trained therapist, you will see the broken pieces in your soul that explain your fear, your confusion, your disposition, and your over-all stuckness. The broken pieces can be glued back together. It can take quite a while. That's why you need a therapist who loves you. Love is the "quite a while" facilitator. Endurance is another true name for love.

The fourth magic key is Expertise. In whatever dream area you are pursuing, there are experts to help you. It takes technical skill to succeed in life. Yes, in some way each expert you consult has a bit of blindness in them. No expert is perfect and Godlike. But when people really know their stuff and have proven track records in their areas, their guidance will save you time; their support and encouragement will strengthen your ego; and their expertise will give you the humility that will remind you that you are possibly an expert too and that even growing experts (like you) always need other experts.

The fifth magic key to success is Action. Like many pro-Secret people said, action is the top necessity that was given short shrift in the video. And action separates the men from the boys, the women from the girls. For example, one day I dreamed of being a psychotherapist. It required lots of action to reach that goal. This included:

Inquiring about psychotherapy schools
Filling out application forms
Going to an initial screening interview
Asking for records from college and graduate school
Obtaining references
Taking lots of classes
Seeing an individual therapist once a week
Seeing two group therapists once a week
Consulting with three supervising therapists once a week
Undergoing 5 hours of critical feedback every 3 months from the above
Recording sessions for feedback
Conducting 3500 hours of therapy for graduation
Writing a thesis
Applying for a job
Learning new skills of marketing, networking, and fee-setting for the business side of therapy
Consulting for ongoing supervision
Continual reading in the field.

Much of this was confusing, difficult, embarrassing, and tiring. Some of it was humiliating. I often felt like giving up. You cannot boil this down to, "I attracted this from the Universe."

Around the same time I did all this, I also dreamed of being a fine golfer. Here is what I have done to that end:

Played golf once a week on an easy course.

Lifted my golf ball out of many sand traps. I hate playing out of sand.

Bought a new set of clubs.

Started to write a book on the creative use of mulligans. (Golf term for a free "do it over").

My golf game has gone down a little, despite my sincere wish to be a better golfer.

The sixth magic key is the magic of Wisdom. Let's use some wisdom in one area of life—the area of self-regard and the marketplace. The lands of capitalism, advertising and big business have a not-very-subtle contempt for ordinary life. If you are a farmer, a single mother, a worker at Walmart, a C student with ADD, or a Hospice nurse, your success so far (though maybe not as dazzling as Cirque de Soleil) deserves a lot more credit RIGHT NOW than you are usually given. But unless things change drastically, the marketplace will never show you the appreciation you deserve.

What we are all saved by is community—the places where everybody knows our name. In our communities there is usually more regard for the "common man" than is found in the elite circles of the world—Wall St., Hollywood, and $25,000 dollar seminars. The purpose of community is to offer a welcome and an embrace to human beings who hate insignificance and loneliness and being excluded.

The magic key of wisdom will keep opening the door to community. Because wisdom knows we need feedback from those who differ with us. Because wisdom knows we need one another. But wisdom will also check out each community to see its weak spots and shortcomings. In a world of amazing complexity, be very suspicious of any group that says it has all the answers.

223

Wisdom is all about dialogue. We move from the monologue of our isolation to the chorus of wisdom.

The seventh magic key is Luck. The Secret is absolutely right about one thing. This is an amazing universe. So we end this chapter with ….the key of luck, which is the unacknowledged key to success.

Let's close with some thoughts about luck and coincidence.

Luck and serendipity and coincidence happen to every group and every person in the world. Coincidence is, therefore, not necessarily the slam-dunk verification of the truth of any belief system. For example, here in abbreviated form are two short stories of amazing coincidence that we have heard about through the years.

An evangelist named Tony Campolo is preaching at a Pentecostal church. The elders of the church lay hands on him and take turns praying for him before the service. One of the elders takes time to pray for a friend of his who is deserting his wife that afternoon. The elder names the guy and tells God where he lives—exit 5 off the Pa. Turnpike, right on White St. into the trailer park, and then the third road on your left and into the second trailer on your right—green trailer with white trim.

In his head, Tony Campolo is wondering why God needs directions, but he commends the friend for his compassion and then joins the rest of the church for worship. After preaching up a storm, Campolo heads home on the Pa. turnpike in the late afternoon and he spots a hitchhiker whom he decides to pick up. They exchange names and Tony suddenly realizes the hitchhiker has the same name as the guy leaving his wife. Tony glances at the suitcases in the back seat and decides that the Lord has done some kind of divine intervention.

So Tony decides to cooperate with the intervention and he reverses direction on the Turnpike and heads for Exit 5, White St., and the green trailer with the white trim.

The hitchhiker's eyes are as wide as marbles when Tony tells him, "I'm taking you back to your wife where God obviously wants you." Last I heard, their marriage was saved and the hitchhiker became a minister and has his own church in California.

Another story: A young Jewish boy rebels from his orthodox Jewish upbringing and goes off to India to learn eastern religions. The father excommunicates his boy from the household and will have nothing to do with him. While in India, the son eventually learns that the father has died and in his grief the son decides to pay more attention to his Jewish heritage. He goes to Israel, sees more of the beauty of his own faith, and also misses his father in a painful way.

He decides to go to the Wailing Wall and write a message in memory of his father. A policeman explains to him they he won't even be able to find a place to leave the message. The son persists and spots what looks like an empty space in some small crevice in the wall. He pushes a little bit to find room and out flutters a piece of paper that has already been jammed in the wall. When it hits the ground, the paper opens up and the son can't help but notice writing that looks very much like his father's. Lo and behold, it turns out that it is a note from his father—explaining his heart-sickness over writing his son off, begging his forgiveness, and hoping that somehow the son will find out about the father's love. The son ended up becoming a Rabbi.

Both stories are touching, uplifting and beautiful. The underlying faith tradition in each story is different, so the fact of coincidence does not prove the truth of every article of each faith. Likewise, if

225

an adoring fan runs into Rhonda Bryne it does not mean The Law of Attraction is a scientific fact.

Nor does coincidence take away all tragedy and make life easy. In the above stories, there were still tears to dry, some explaining to do, graves to visit and the minister still had to learn Greek and the Rabbi still had to learn Hebrew.

What goes on the most in both stories is action—the movement of people wishing and hoping, yes, but then, even more, the movement of following those desires with driving and traveling and writing and being open to possibility. It's sort of like Vegas and the Lottery. You can't win if you don't play. Coincidence favors movement.

So we all need much more than coincidence and a feeling state.

The material success of The Secret comes from the fact that people like the Hicks and Rhonda Bryne left their chairs and sofas. They had the courage to share what they think is their best for the world. They did not just attract it in an easy way. It has taken a lot of movement to get to where they are. We can see the pens writing, the cameras rolling, the phone calls made, the bills paid, and the RV rolling down the road to another seminar.

We wish good luck to all involved with The Secret—whether pro or con.

Unlike the advocates of The Secret, we cannot guarantee this will happen. But we can guarantee that it is our wish for you.

Bibliography

Abraham, Jay. 2000. *Getting Everything You Can Out of All You've Got*. New York: St. Martins Press.

Adler, Jerry. 2007. *Decoding the Secret*. Newsweek. March 5.

Atkinson, William Walker. 1906. *Thought Vibration or the Law of Attraction in the Thought World*. New Thought Publishing Co.

Barth, Karl. 1957. *Church Dogmatics* Vol. 3, Pt. 4. Edinburgh: T&T Clark.

Beverley, Bob.2007. *How To Be A Christian and Still Be Sane*. New York. IUniverse.

Beverley, James A. 2005. *Religions A to Z*. Nashville. Thomas Nelson.

Bloom, Harold. 2002. *Genius*. New York. Warner Books.

Byrne, Rhonda. 2006. *The Secret*. New York. Atria Books.

Brooks, Phillips. 1899. *Lectures on Preaching*. New York: Dutton.

Buechner, Frederick. 1977. *Telling the Truth*. San Francisco: Harper & Row.

———. 1982. *The Sacred Journey*. San Francisco: Harper &

227

Row.

———. 1983. *Now and Then.* San Francisco: Harper & Row.

———. 1984. *The Book of Bebb.* New York: Atheneum

———. 1991. *Telling Secrets.* New York: Harper Collins.

———. 1999. *Eyes of the Heart.* New York: Harper Collins.

Capon, Robert Farrar. 1965. *Bed and Board.* New York: Simon & Schuster.

———. 1967. *Supper of the Lamb.* New York: Doubleday.

Dawkins, Richard. 2006. *The God Delusion.* Boston. Houghton Mifflin.

Doyle, Bob. 2003. *Wealth Beyond Reason.* Victoria, B.C. Canada. Trafford Publishing.

Eliot, John. 2004. *Overachievement.* New York. Penguin Books.

Fine, Cordelia. 2006. *A Mind of its Own: How Your Brain Distorts and Deceives.* New York, NY: W.W. Norton & Company.

Freud, Sigmund. 1989. *Civilization and its Discontents.* New York, NY: W.W. Norton & Company.

Gibran, Kahil. 1994. *The Prophet.* New York: Alfred A. Knopf.

Gilbert, Daniel. *Stumbling on Happiness*, New York, NY: Alfred A. Knopf, 2006

Gracian, Balthasar. 1993. *The Art of Worldly Wisdom.* New York: Shambhala.

Grudin, Robert. 1982. *Time and the Art of Living.* New York: Harper & Row.

Hallowell, Edward M. 1997. *Worry: Hope and Help for a Common Condition.* New York: Ballantine Books.

Hepburn, Ronald W. 1955. *Christianity and Paradox.* New York. Pegasus.

Hicks, Esther and Jerry. 2006. *The Law of Attraction.* Carlsbad, California. Hay House.

Hills, L. Rust. 1972. *How to Do Things Right.* Boston: David R. Godine.

Hoffer, Eric. 1955. *The Passionate State of Mind.* New York: Harper & Row.

Hogan, Kevin, and James Speakman. 2006. *Covert Persuasion.* Hoboken, NJ: John Wiley & Sons.

Hollon, Frank Turner. 2002. *The God File.* San Francisco: MacAdam/Cage Publishing.

Howard, Thomas. 1967. *Christ the Tiger.* New York: J. B. Lippincott & Co.

————. 1969. *An Antique Drum.* New York: J. B. Lippincott & Co.

————. 1976. *Splendor in the Ordinary.* Wheaton, IL: Tyndale.

Irving, John. 2002. *A Prayer for Owen Mean.* New York: Modern Library.

Joyner, Mark. 2007. *simple.ology*. Hoboken, NJ. John Wiley and Sons.

Lakhani, Dave. 2005. *Persuasion: The Art of Getting What You Want*. Hoboken, NJ: John Wiley & Sons.

Lamott, Anne. 1994. *Bird by Bird*. New York: Anchor Books. *Larry King Live*, March 8, 2007

Lear, Jonathan. 1990. *Love and Its Place in Nature*. New York: Farrar, Straus and Giroux.

Lewis, C. S. 1940. *The Problem of Pain*. London: Collins.

———. 1943. *Mere Christianity*. New York: MacMillan Publishing.

———. 1946. *The Great Divorce*. New York: MacMillan Publishing.

_____. 1947. *Miracles*. Glasgow. William Collins and Sons.

———. 1955 *Surprised by Joy*. London: HarperCollins.

Lloyd-Jones, David Martyn. 1965. *Spiritual Depression: Its Causes and Cure*. Grand Rapids, MI: William B. Eerdmans.

Losier, Michael J. 2006 *Law of Attraction*. Victoria, B.C. Canada. Michael J. Losier.

Mack, Ben. 2007. *Think Two Products Ahead: Secrets the Big Advertising Agencies Don't Want You to Know and How to Use Them for Bigger Profits*. Hoboken, NJ: John Wiley & Sons.

Mackay, Harvey. 2005. *Fired Up!: How the Best of the Best Survived and Thrived After Getting the Boot.* New York, Ballantine Books.

Martel, Yanni. 2001. *Life of Pi.* New York: Harcourt.

Maslow, Abraham. 1998. *Toward a Psychology of Being.* New York: Wiley.

Mastropolo, Frank. 2006. *'The Secret' to Success?* ABCNews.com. November 26.

Milgram, Stanley. 1974. *Obedience to Authority.* New York, NY, Harper & Row.

Mishlove, Jeffrey. *The High and the Low with Colin Wilson.*

Thinking Allowed, Conversations On the Leading Edge of Knowledge and Discovery. The Intuition Network.

Murdoch, Iris. 1977. *The Fire and The Sun.* Oxford. Oxford University Press.

_____. 1968. *The Nice and The Good.* New York. Penguin Books.

National Council of Churches of the USA, Division of Christian Education. 1971. *Harper Study Bible: The Holy Bible, RSV.* Grand Rapids, MI: Zondervan Corporation.

Neuhaus, Richard John. 2000. *Death on a Friday Afternoon.* New York: Basic Books.

Nightline, ABC. March 23, 2007

NobelPrize.org – John Hume Nobel Lecture, December 10, 1998

Oprah, February 8, 2007

Oprah, March 26, 2007

Pagels, Heinz R. 1983. *The Cosmic Code: Quantum Physics as the Language of Nature*. New York, NY: Bantam Books.

Peck, M. Scott. 1978. *The Road Less Traveled*. New York: Simon & Schuster.

People – March 19, 2007

Phillips, Michael. 1970. *The Seven Laws of Money*. New York: Random House.

Pittman, Frank. 1987. *Turning Points*. New York. W. W. Norton.

Plato. 1961. *The Collected Dialogues of Plato*. Princeton. Princeton University Press.

Ray, James Arthur. 2006. *The Science of Success*. Carlsbad, California. Sunark Press.

Ray, James Arthur. *JamesRay.com.*

Remnick, David. 2000. *Cornerman*. The New Yorker. August 21 & 28.

Reynolds, David K. 1984. *Constructive Living*. Honolulu, Hawaii: University of Hawaii Press.

Richardson Jr., Robert D. 1995. *Emerson: The Mind on Fire*. Berkeley. Univ. of California Press.

Rutherford, Darel. 1998. *So, Why Aren't You Rich?* Albuquergue, NM. Dar Publishing.

Sagan, Carl. 1997. *The Demon Haunted World: Science as a Candle in the Dark.* New York, NY: Ballantine Books.

Salkin, Allen. 2007. *Shaking Riches Out of the Cosmos.*

New York Times. Feb. 25.

Schiffman, Nathaniel. 2005. *Abracadabra: Secret Methods Magicians & Others Use to Deceive Their Audience.* Amherst, New York: Prometheus Books.

Schnarch, David. 1991. *Constructing the Sexual Crucible.* New York: W. W. Norton.

Sheed, Wilfred. 1995. *In Love with Daylight.* New York: Simon & Schuster.

Stossel, John. 2007. *Scared Stiff - Worry in America.* ABC. February 23.

Sulivan, Jean. 1976. *Morning Light.* New York: Paulist Press.

Taylor, Barbara Brown. 2006. *Leaving Church: A Memoir of Faith.* San Francisco: HarperCollins.

The Secret (Extended Edition). 2006. Prod. Rhonda Byrne. DVD. Prime Time Productions.

The Secret (Original Edition). 2006. Prod. Rhonda Byrne. DVD. Prime Time Productions.

TheSecret.tv. *Official Website of The Secret Movie.*

ThinkExist.com

Toumey, Christopher P. 1996. *Conjuring Science: Scientific Symbols and Cultural Meanings in American Life*. New Brunswick, New Jersey: Rutgers University Press.

Updike, John. 1989. *Self-Consciousness*. New York: Alfred A. Knopf.

Vitale, Joe. 2005. *The Attractor Factor*. Hoboken, N.J. John Wiley and Sons

Warren, Blair. 2007. *The Law of Extraction Revealed*. BlairWarren.com. February 27.

Wegner, Daniel M. 1989. *White Bears and Other Unwanted Thoughts: Suppression, Obsession, and the Psychology of Mental Control*. New York, NY: Penguin Books.

WhatisTheSecret.tv

What-is-the-Secret.blogspot.com

Wheelis, Allen. 1967. *The Doctor of Desire*. New York: W. W. Norton & Co.

———. 1973. *How People Change*. New York: Harper & Row.

Wilkinson, Bruce. 2000. *The Prayer of Jabez*. Sisters, Oregon. Multnomah Publishers.

Wilson, Timothy D. 2002. *Strangers to Ourselves: Discovering the Adaptive Unconscious*. Cambridge, Massachusetts: The Belknap Press of Harvard University Press.

Winget, Larry. 2004. Shut Up, Stop Whining & Get a Life: A Kick-Butt Approach to a Better Life. New York: John Wiley & Sons.

World News with Charles Gibson. ABC. March 16, 2007.

Wynn, Charles M. and Arthur W. Wiggins. 2001. *Quantum Leaps in the Wrong Direction: Where Real Science Ends and Pseudoscience Begins.* Washington D.C. Joseph Henry Press.

THE SECRET BEHIND THE SECRET LAW OF ATTRACTION

Bob Beverley
Dave Lakhani
Blair Warren
Kevin Hogan

Bob Beverley is a psychotherapist and Co-Director of Northeast Counseling Center in New York State. He is the author of *How To Be A Christian And Still Be Sane*. His expertise comes from 25 years of pastoral ministry and 26,000 hours of psychotherapy work. Bob has a B.A. in Philosophy and English Literature, an M.Div. in Philosophy of Religion, and a postgraduate degree in individual and marital psychotherapy. Visit his website, FindWisdomNow.com, and download a free copy of the E book, "The Power of Fear".

Dave Lakhani is a recognized expert on persuasion, propaganda, mass influence and building cults of customers. Dave was raised in a strict religious cult based on the teachings of William Branham until his late teens.

For the past 25 years Dave has studied persuasion, influence, marketing, advertising, propaganda, mass movements, and the psychology of change. He has applied those ideas to help more than 1000 different companies in scores of different industries transform their business and accelerate their sales and profitability.

Dave is an in demand speaker who addresses thousands of people worldwide each year and regularly appears on the largest platforms in the world. His unique blend of real world experience, storytelling, and content that can be implemented immediately keeps audiences on the edge of their seat.

A regular in the media, you've seen Dave in Sales and Marketing Management, The Wall Street Journal, Fortune, Wealth, Inc., Entrepreneur, The Today Show, CNN, and literally hundreds of newspapers around the world. Dave was the host of the long running radio program The Business Connection. For more information about Dave visit www.boldapproach.com.

Blair Warren is a television producer, writer, marketing consultant and a self-described voracious student of human nature. For over three decades he has immersed himself in ideas from areas as diverse as psychology, philosophy, enlightenment, persuasion, marketing, magic (as in tricks), Magick (as in the Occult), scams, con games and more. He is the author of *The Forbidden Keys to Persuasion* and *Enlighten This!* (available summer 2007, Kallisti Publishing). His website is at www.blairwarren.com.

Kevin Hogan is a dynamic, well-known international motivational and inspirational keynote speaker, consultant and corporate trainer. He has trained persuasion, sales and marketing skills to leaders in the government of Poland, employees from Boeing, Microsoft, Starbucks, and numerous other Fortune 500 companies.

Kevin is the author of more than twelve books, including, *The Science of Influence, The Psychology of Persuasion and Irresistible Attraction*. He is often called the "go to" influence and persuasion consultant. He has shared his specialized knowledge in persuasion and influence with the New York Times, CNN, the BBC, Fox Television, and dozens of popular magazines like

Cosmopolitan, First for Women, Woman's World, Playboy, Women's Own, Redbook, King, Maxim, Stuff, Selling Power and others.

His keynotes, seminars and workshops help companies sell, market and communicate more effectively. His cutting edge research into the mind and keen understanding of consumer behavior create a unique distillation of information never before released to the public.

To make Kevin Hogan the dynamic speaker (read that as *very dynamic, funny, informative and knock 'em dead!)* for your next event, go to www.kevinhogan.net.

"*We measure ourselves by many standards. Our strength and our intelligence, our wealth and even our good luck, are things which warm our heart and make us feel ourselves a match for life. But deeper than all such things and able to suffice unto itself without them, is the sense of the amount of effort we can put forth....He who can make none is but a shadow; he who can make much is a hero.*"
--William James

Printed in the United States
109447LV00002B/86/A

9 781934 266021